Diary of Brave Rave (Baby) - Coloring Book

978-0-9973598-9-3

❋ Flower Press LLC
St. Louis, MO
BraveRaveBook.com

THANK YOU

to all the people who have been part
of this amazing experience–the good, the bad and the ALL. I want to
give a special thanks to my friends, family, teachers and mentors who
continued to encourage me to Image and Grow through this journey.

May we all
IMAGINE & GROW

The world is ours.
Take a Moment to Give back.

Diary of Baby Brave Rave

Coloring Book

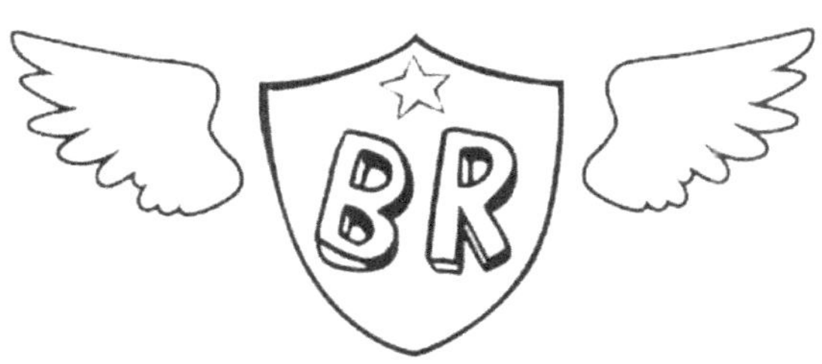

by Raquel Hunter

Flower Press Publishing

ABOUT THE AUTHOR

Raquel Hunter is a real-life **Diva Mom**, so she is perfectly qualified to write the **BRAVERAVE** book series. In fact, she's been seen writing this book wearing the cutest pink yoga pants and flip-flops that have more bling than the Queen of England's tiara.

More than anything else in the world, Raquel believes that little girls can grow up to do amazing things. After all, she joined the Navy when she was 17 years old and got to live in Japan during her four-year tour of duty. After that, she got a degree in social work and became a youth mentor. She has also designed purses and made candles.

These days, when she is not writing Brave Rave books or teaching yoga she is doing her most important job — being Raven's mom.

Raquel lives in St. Louis with her diva-in- training-daughter Raven and her husband, the **DO-IT-ALL DAD**.

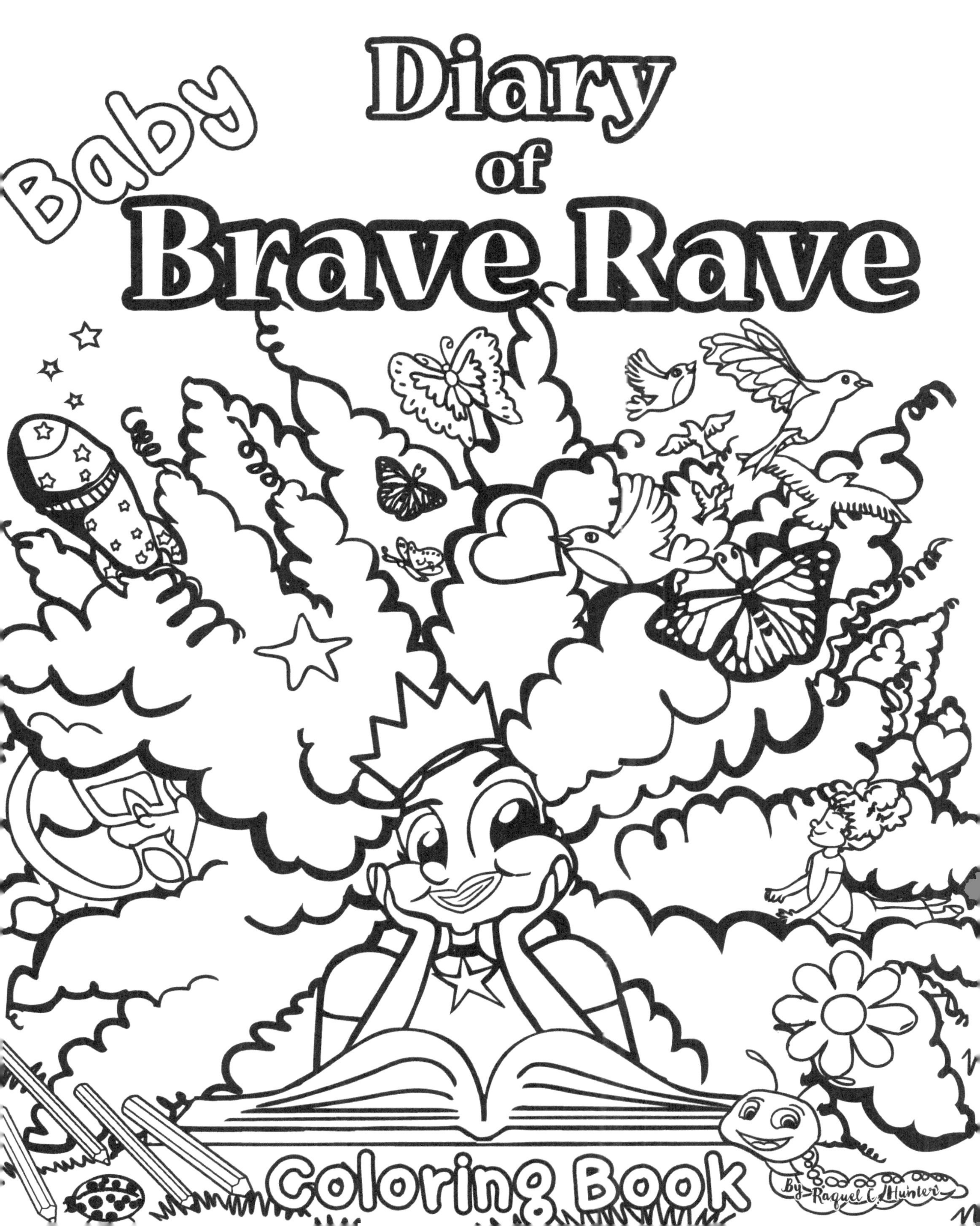

Baby
Diary
of
Brave Rave
Coloring Book
By>Raquel C. Hunter

Mom & Dad are always saying that I grow soooooo fast.

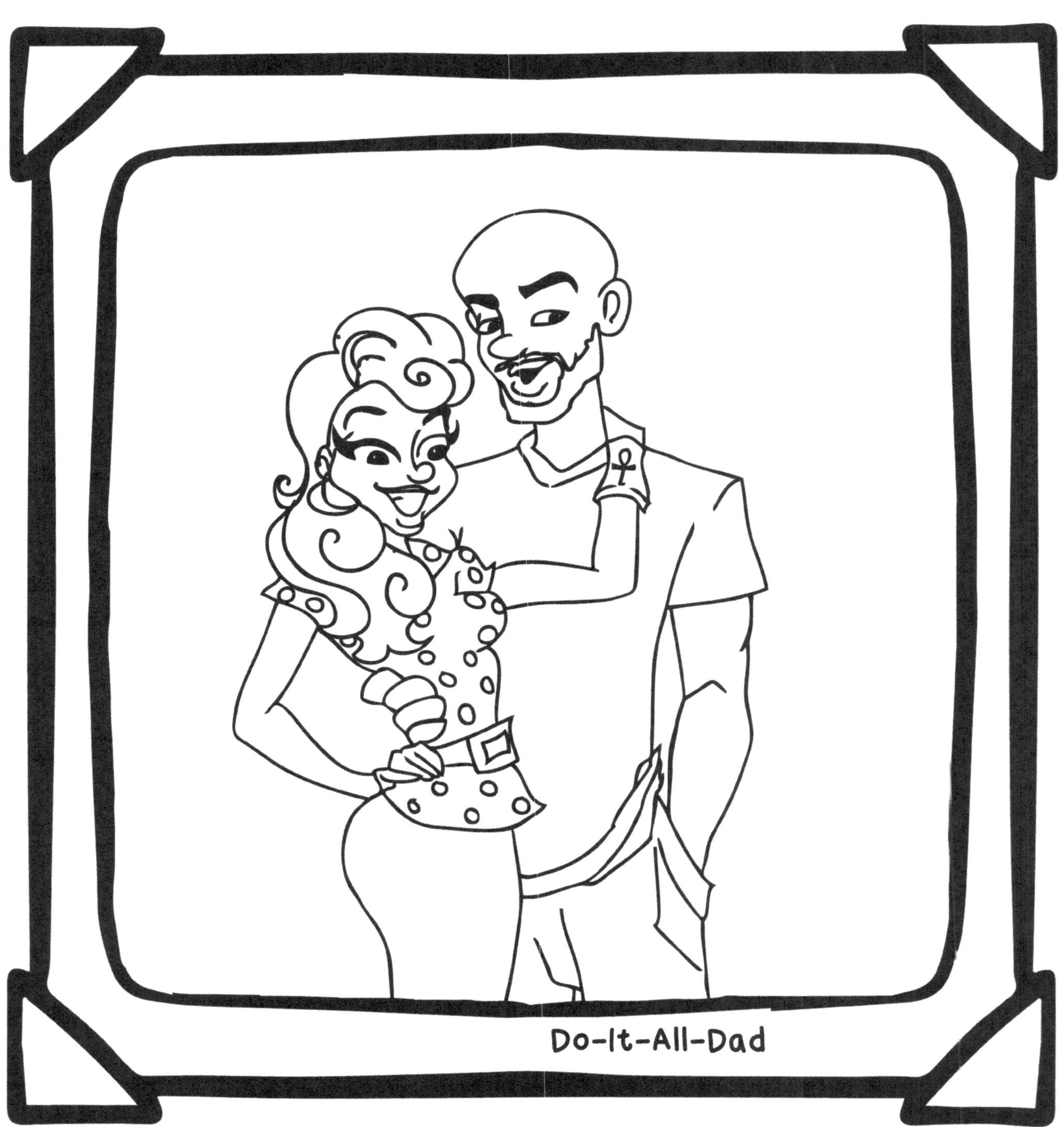

Do-It-All-Dad

They say every time they BLINK, I GROW.

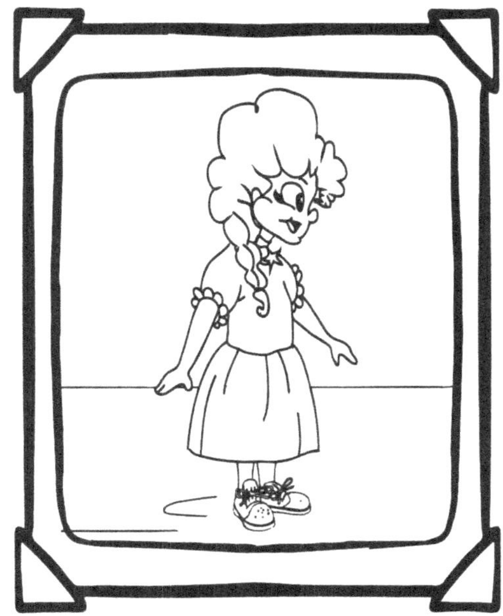

Brave Rave
at 3 years old

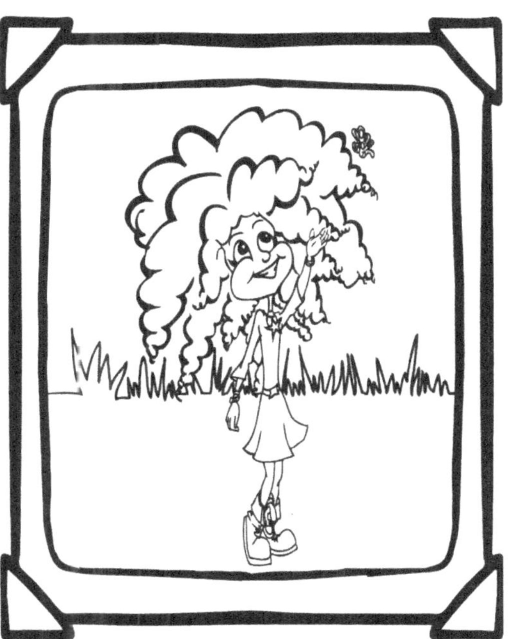

Brave Rave
at 8 years old

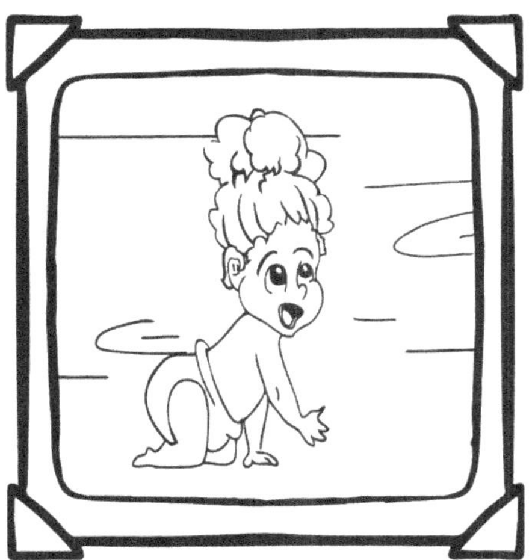

Brave Rave
at 6 months old

I can remember, smiling
at the moon and reaching
for the stars as a baby.

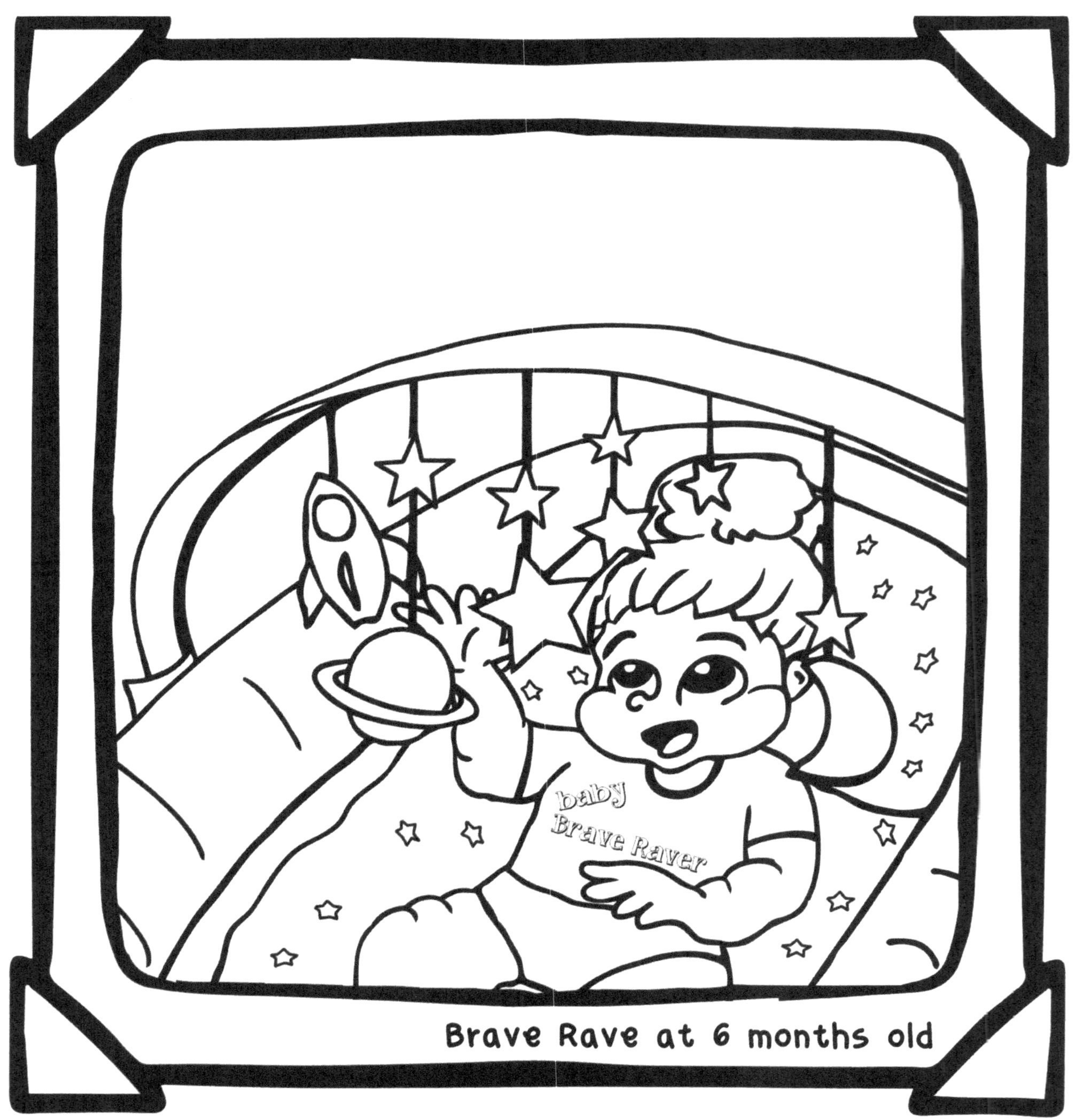

Brave Rave at 6 months old

IMAGINE

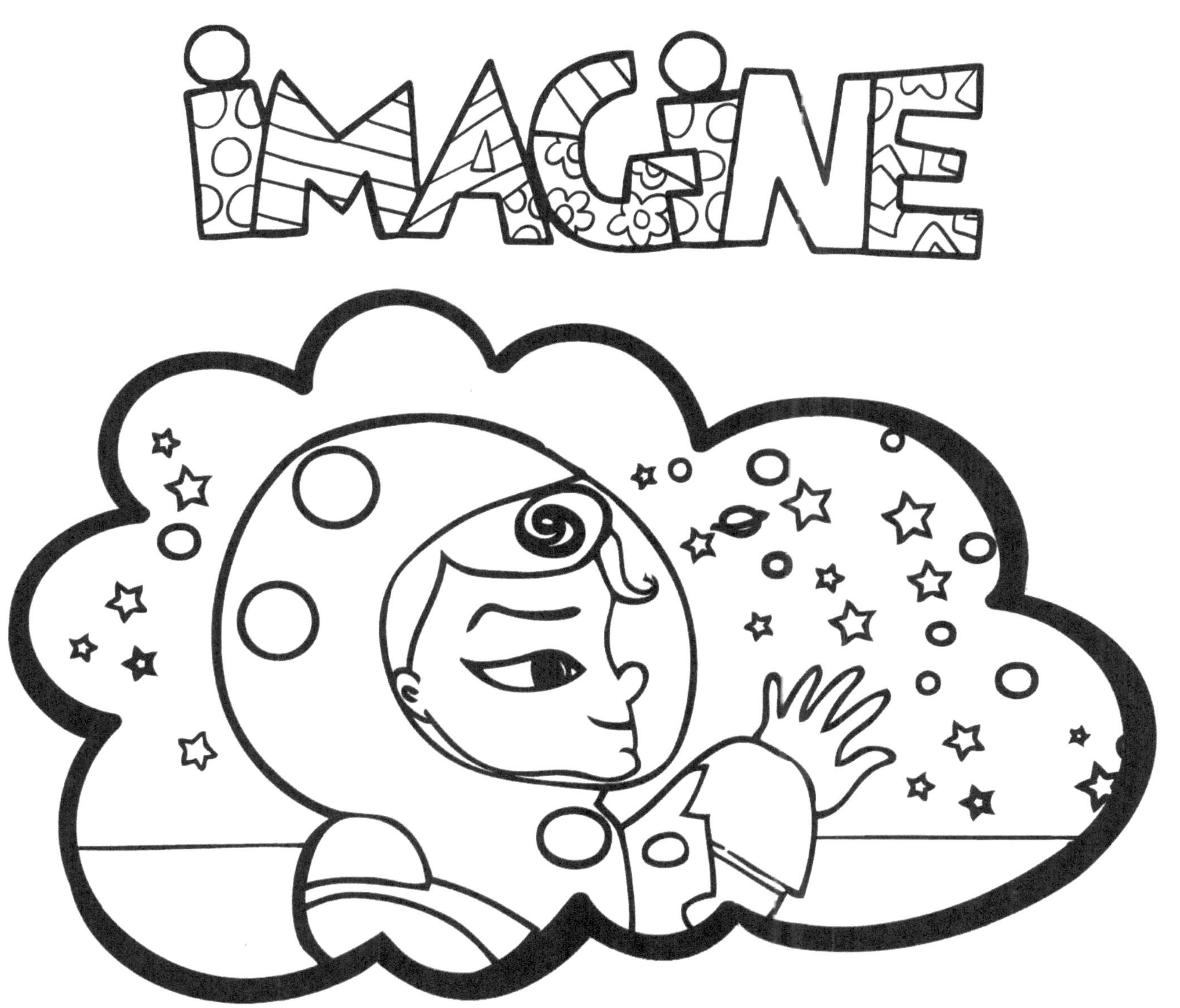

being an astronaut
exploring the moons,
planets, and stars of
other worlds.

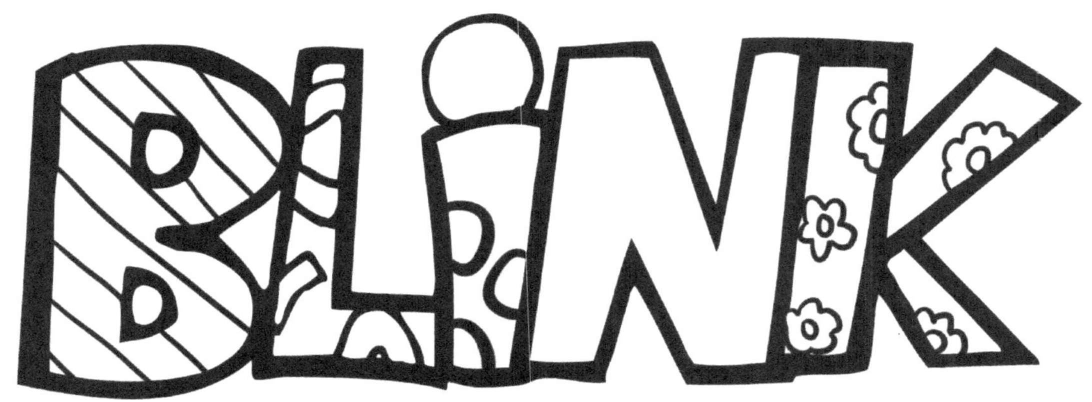
BLINK

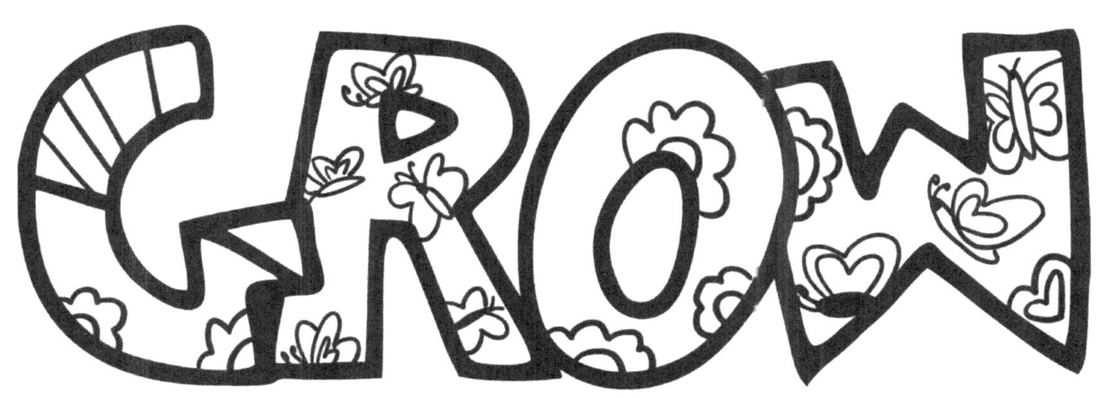

GROW

I join Mom in a nice yoga stretch because it is good for relaxing your mind and your body. Mom says it helps me to be my very BEST.

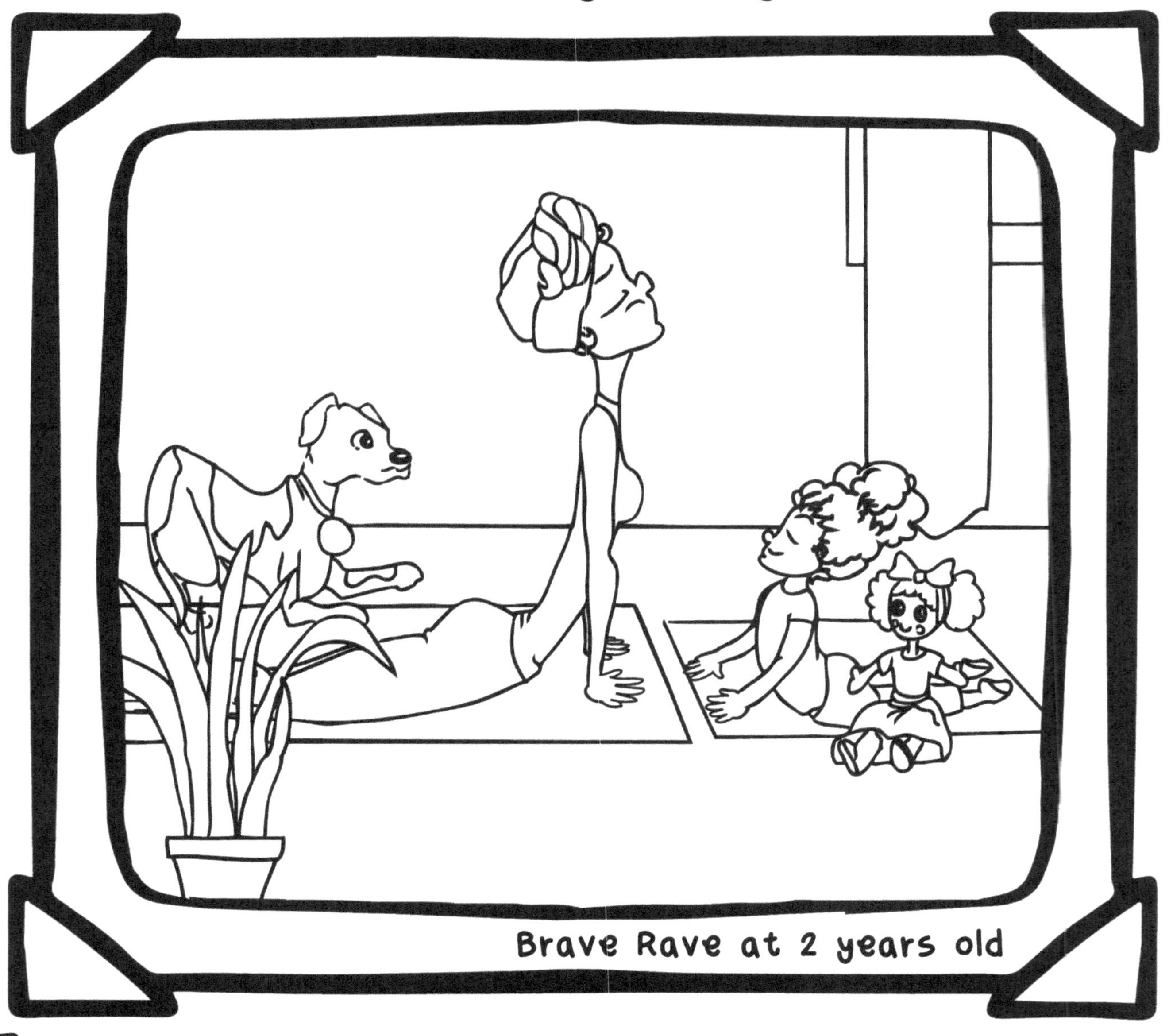

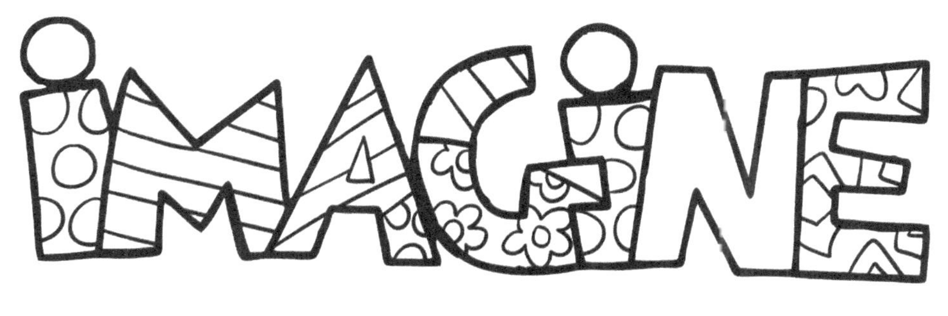

love, peace, laughter,
strawberries, melons, warm
breezes, cookies, cupcakes, stars,
beetles, unicorns & butterflies
and everything Happy!!

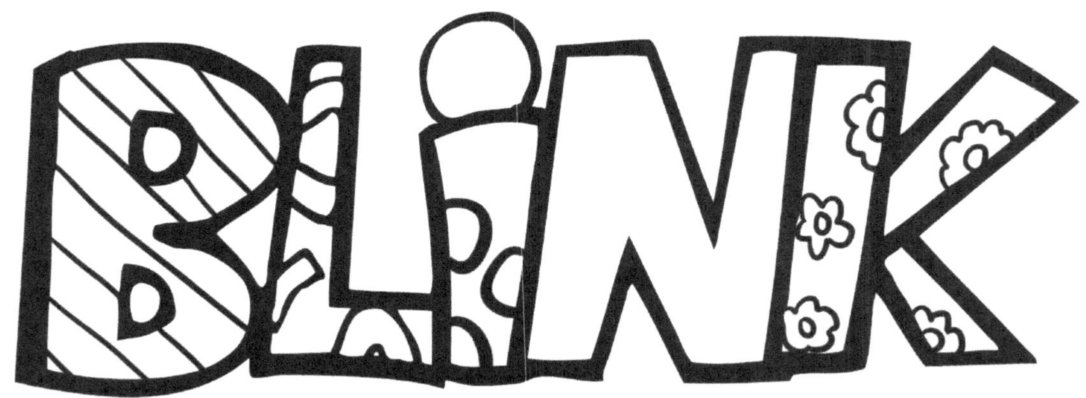
BLINK

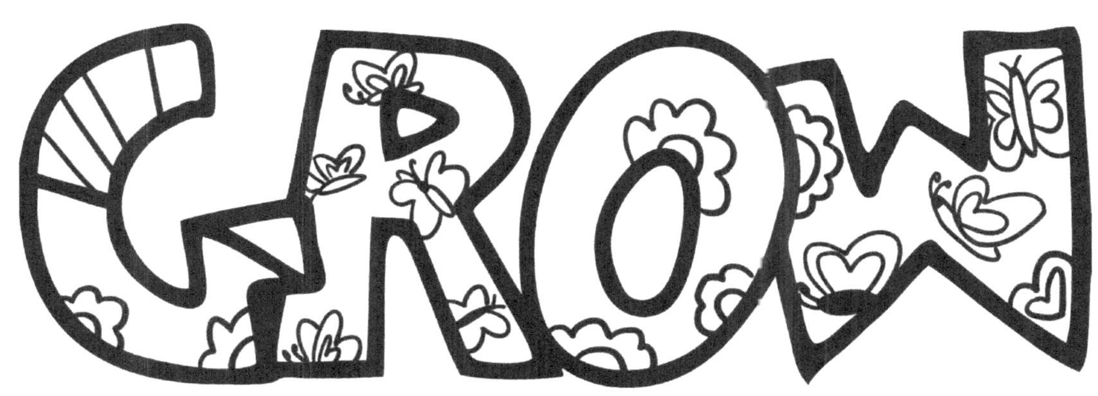
GROW

I tumble, twist,
turn, bend and flip
all over my room.

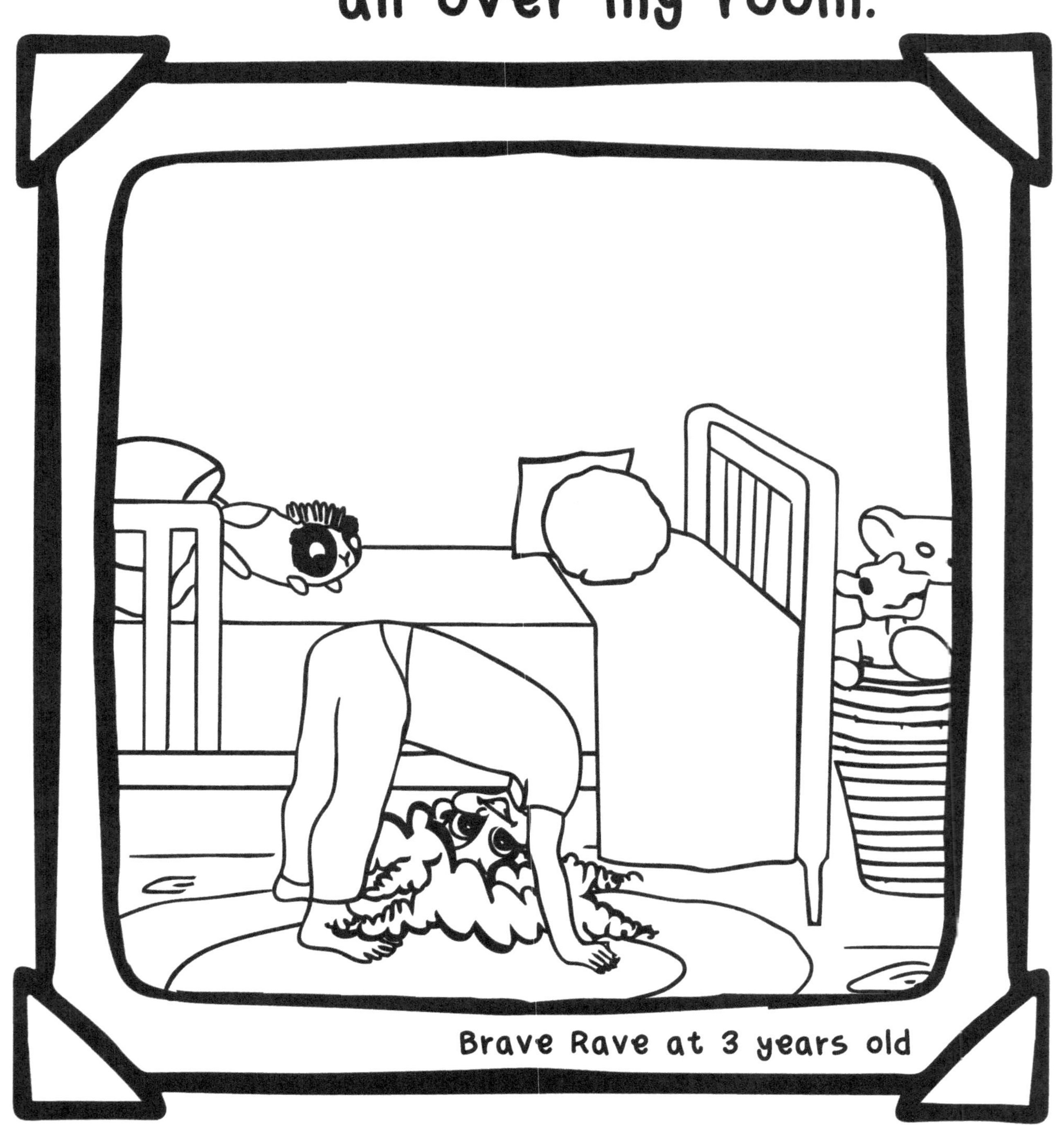

Brave Rave at 3 years old

IMAGINE

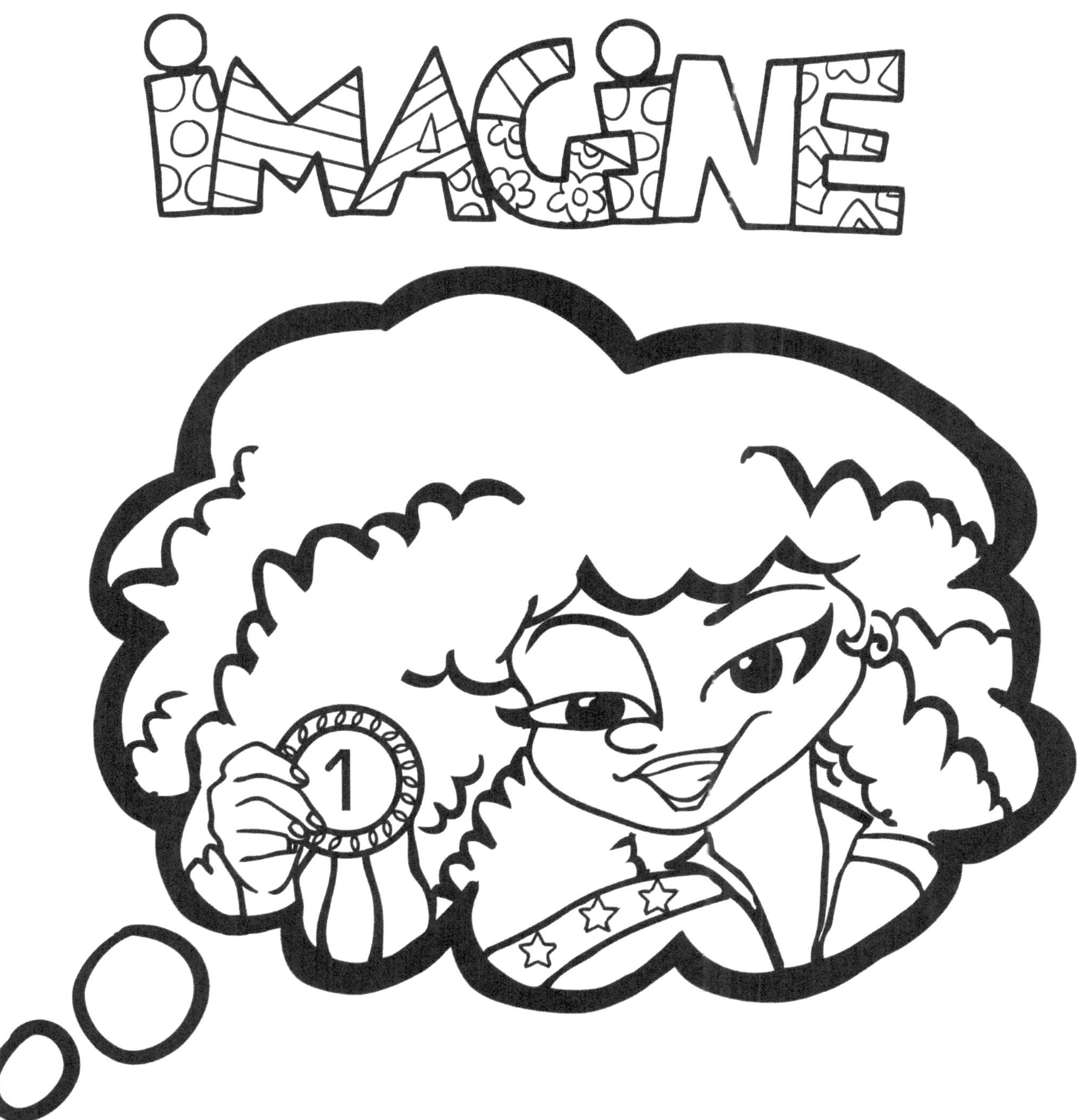

tumbling for a living and being
the very best Olympic gymnast
in the entire world!

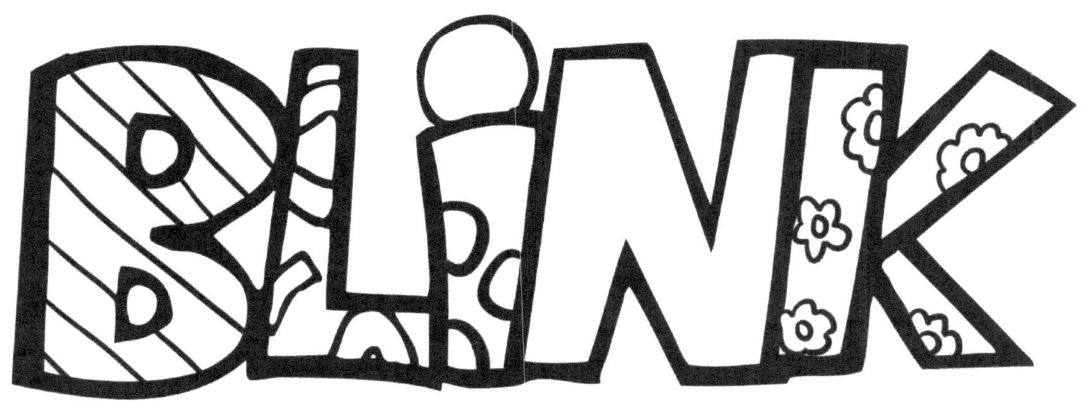

13

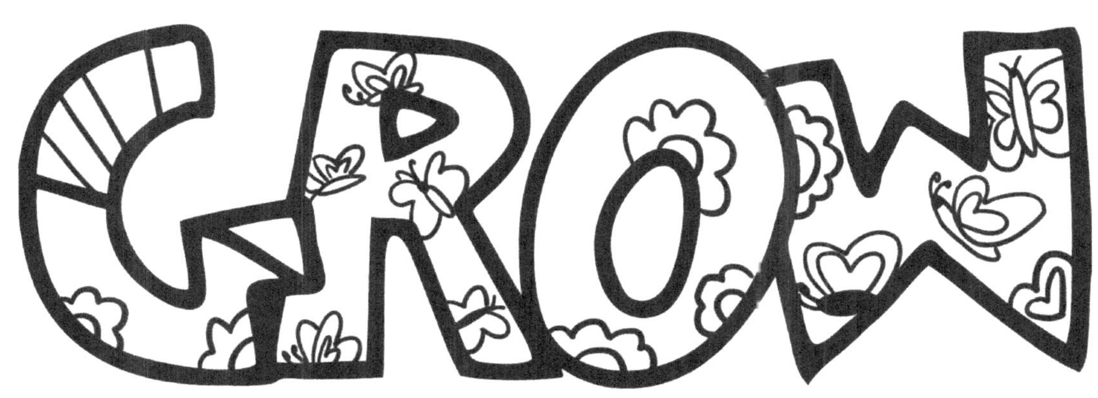
GROW

I go to the bathroom to brush, brush, brush, brush my teeth so they can be clean and sparkly.

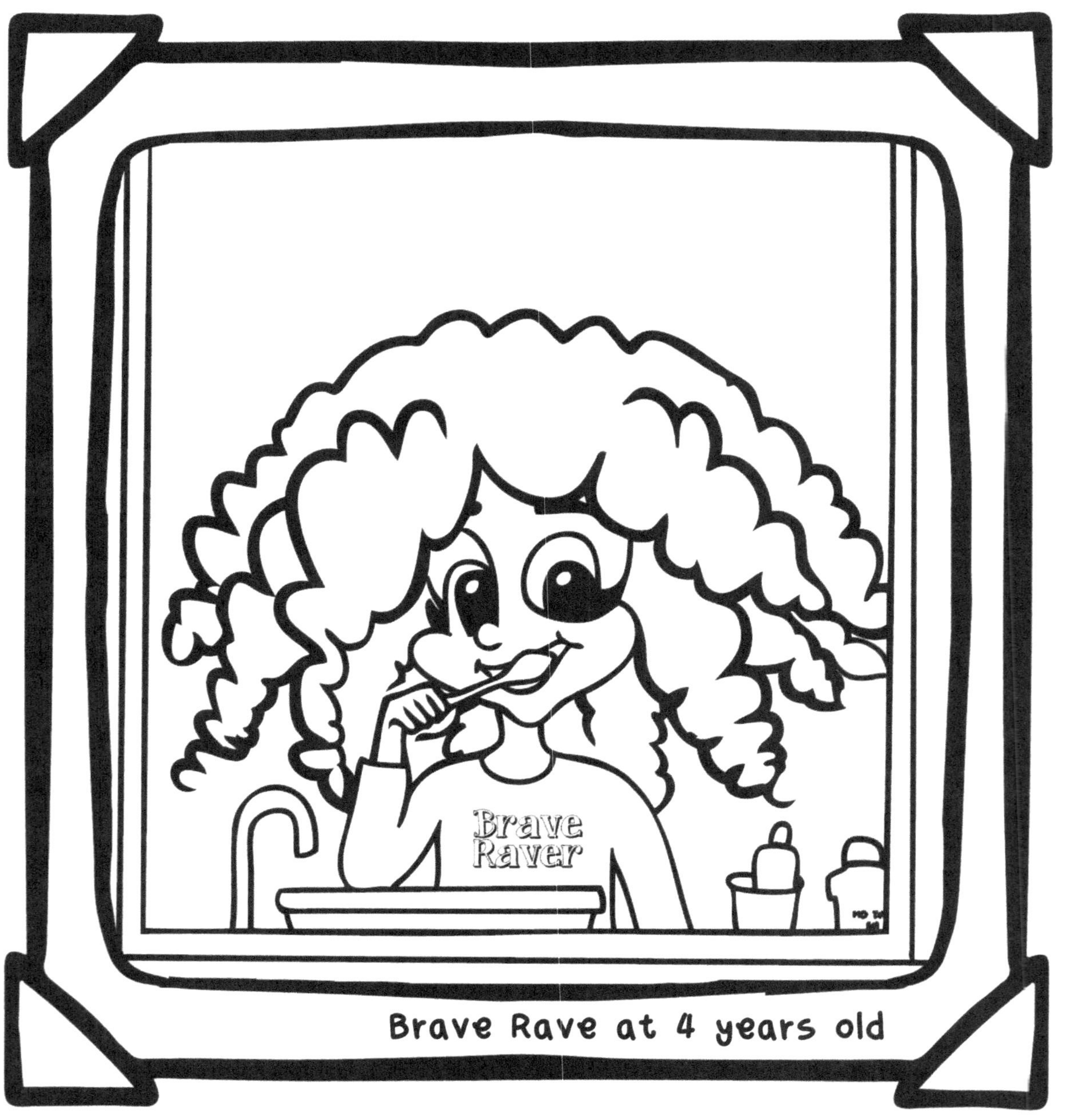

Brave Rave at 4 years old

IMAGINE

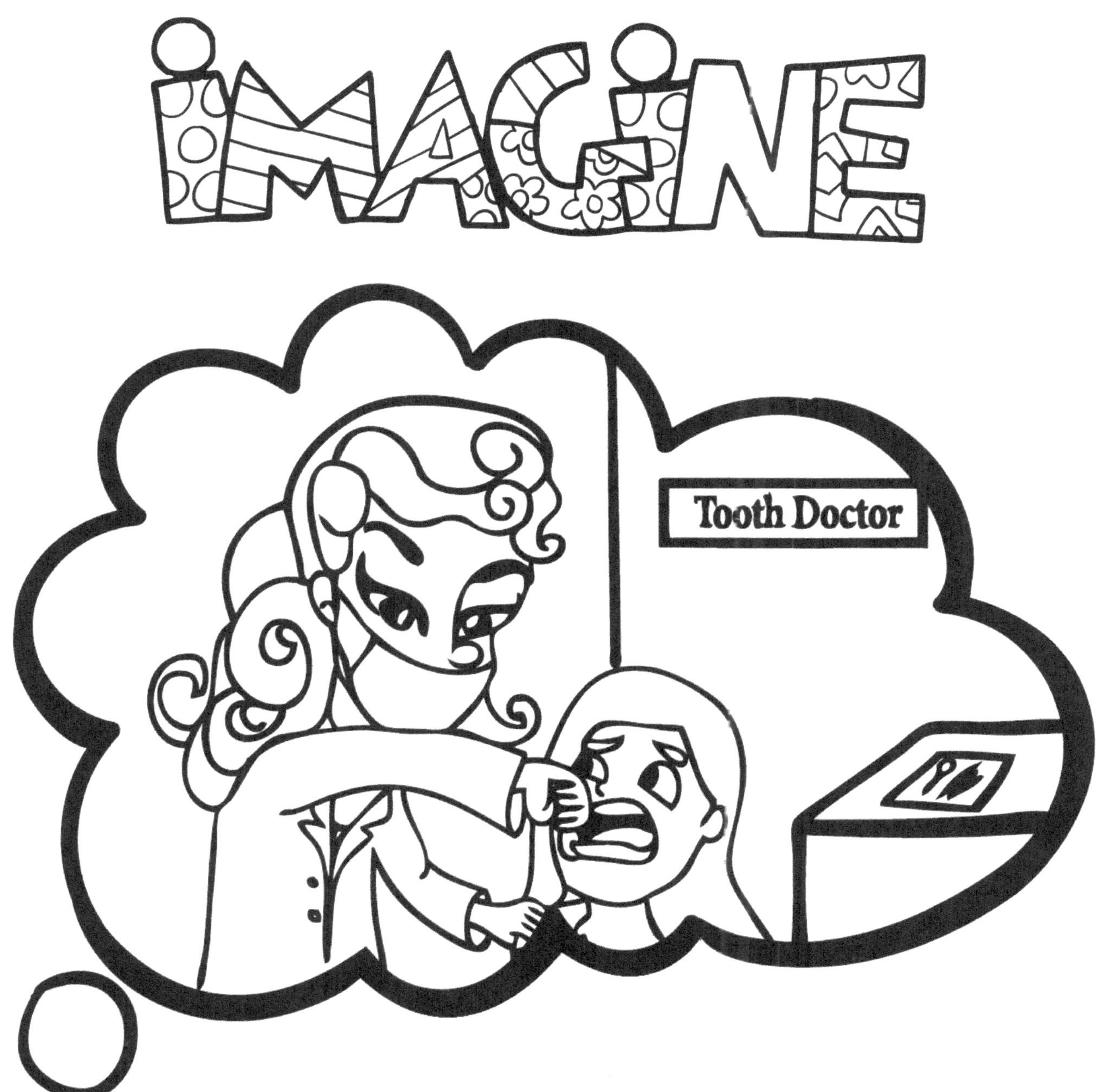

being a super awesome
dentist that helps people keep
their teeth clean and healthy.

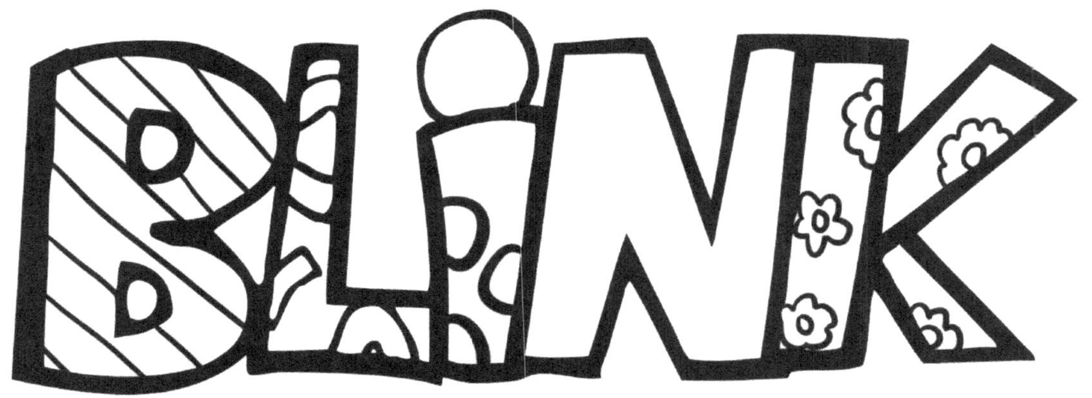
BLINK

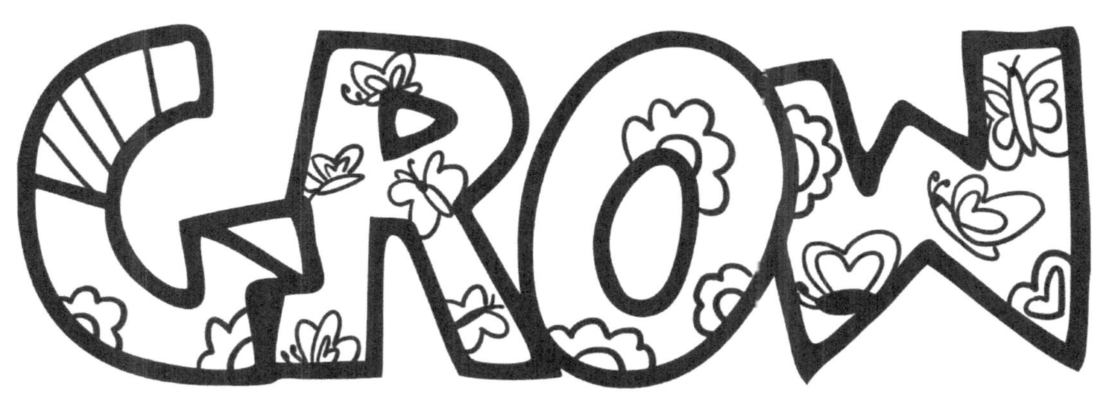

GROW

I have a great time as I
splash-splash-splash in the bath.
I must also keep clean and wash
the day's dirt from my body.

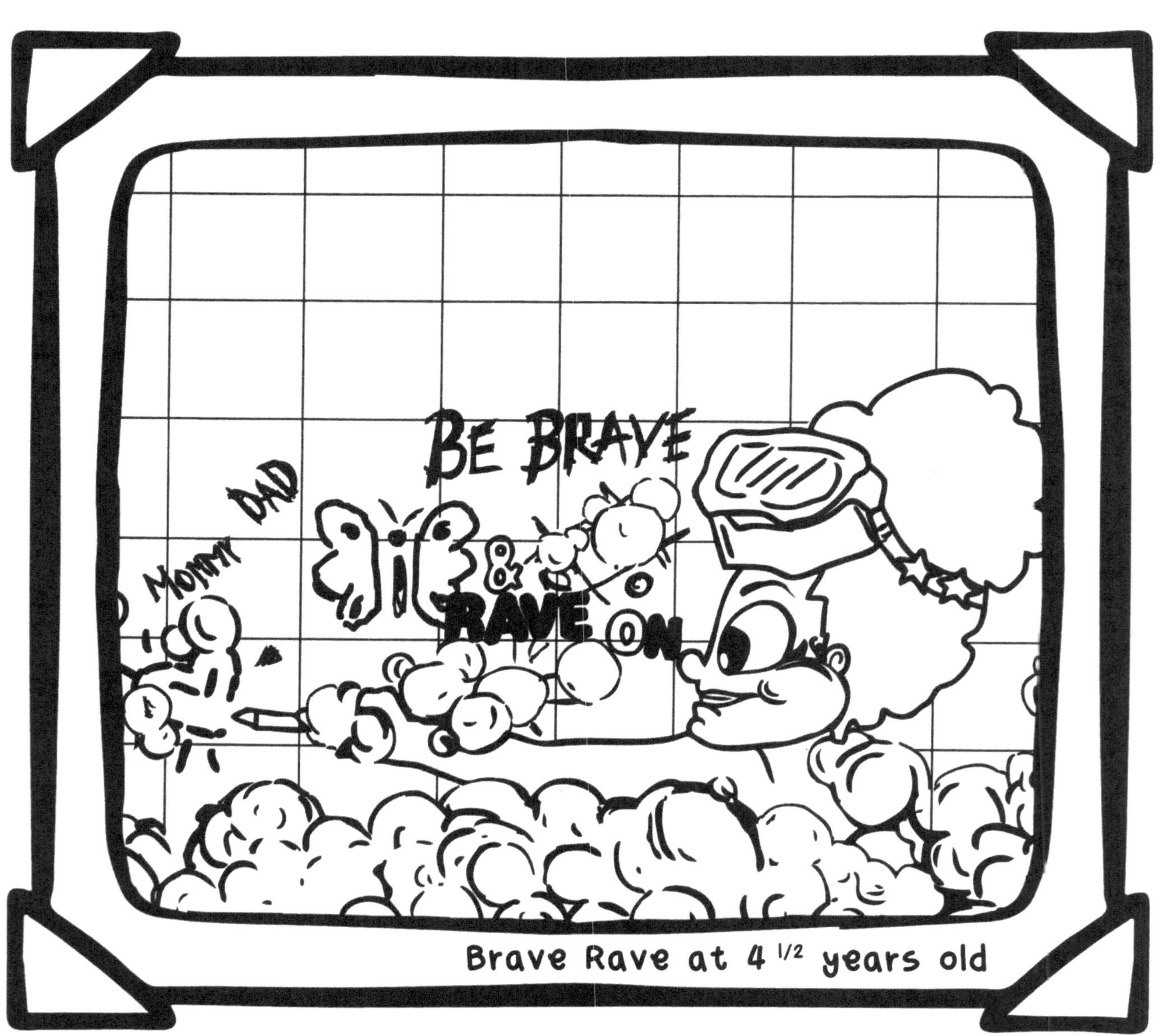

Brave Rave at 4 1/2 years old

IMAGINE

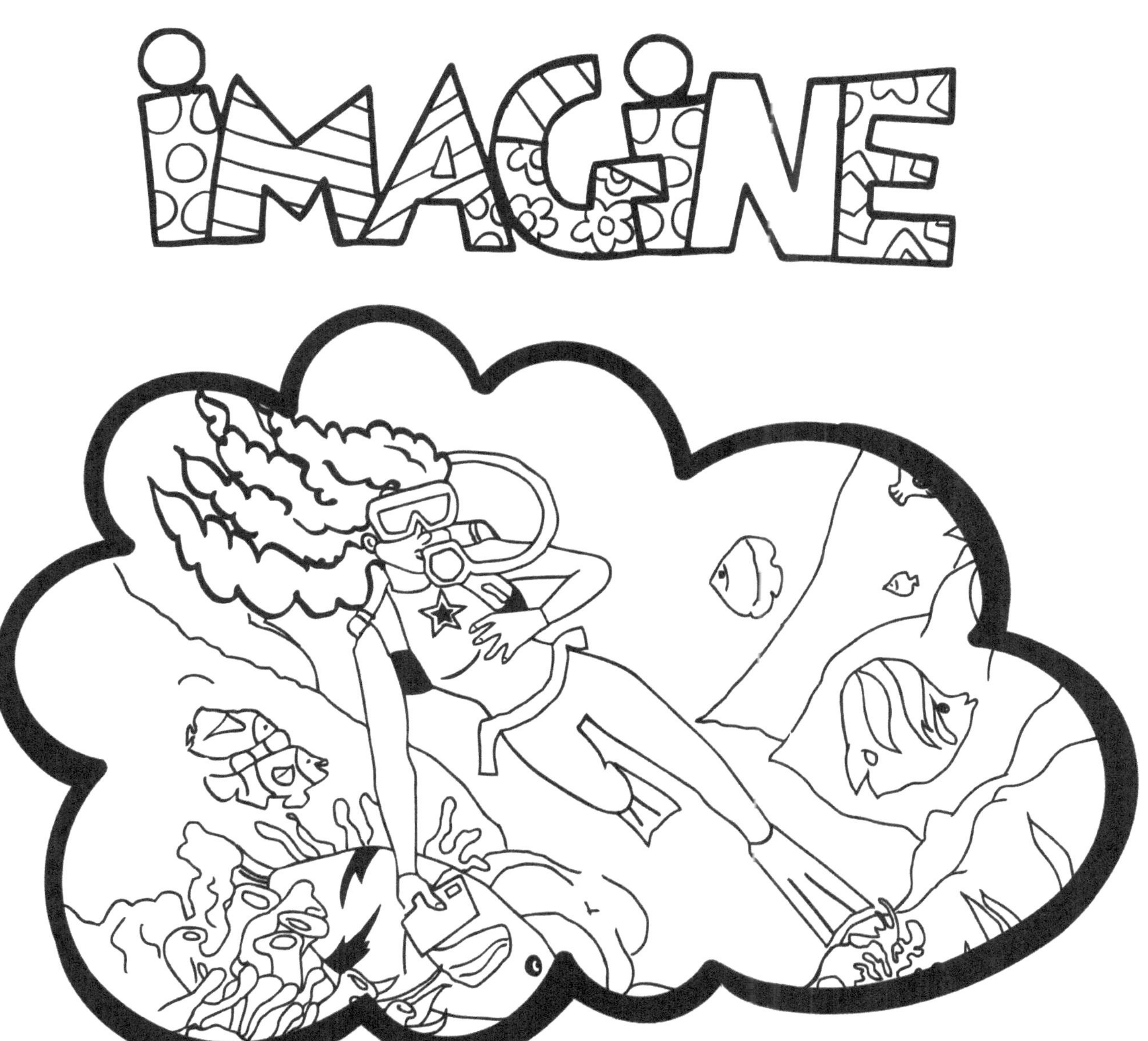

being a marine biologist
and splashing in the ocean
studying and discovering
amazing creatures of the sea.

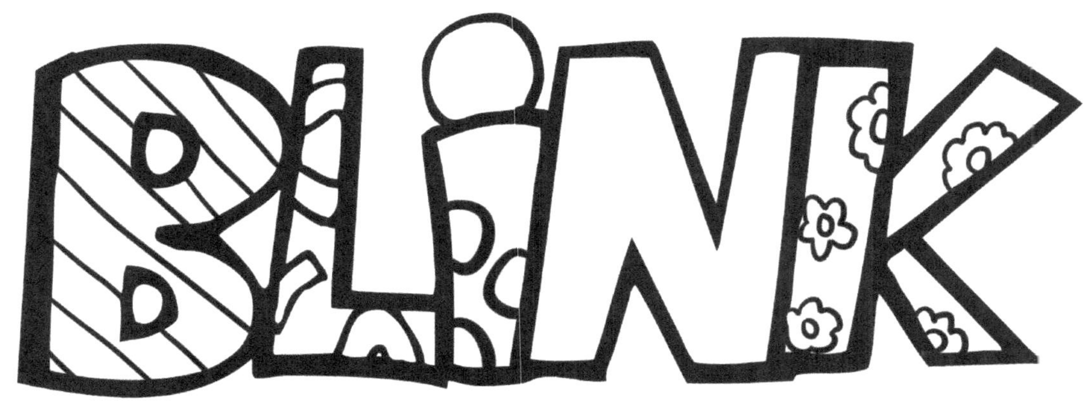

21

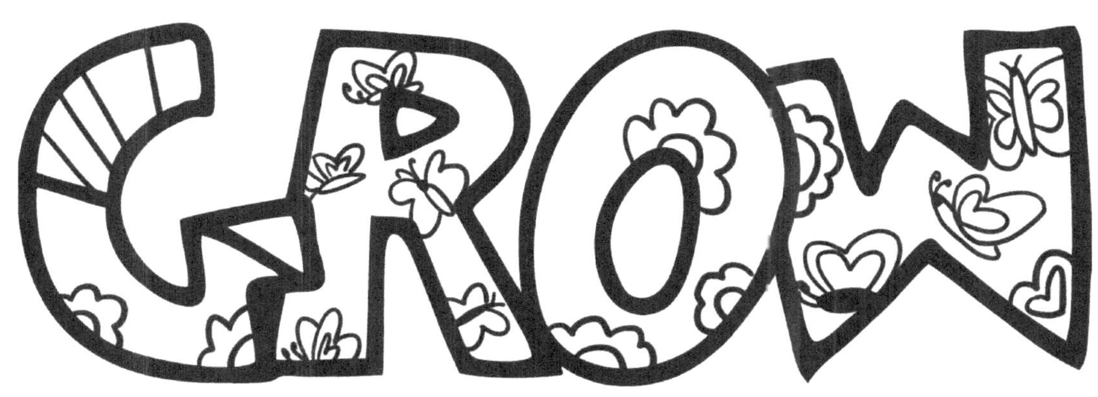

GROW

I grab my paper, pencil,
and crayons to draw-draw-
draw-draw because it is fun.
Drawing makes me happy.

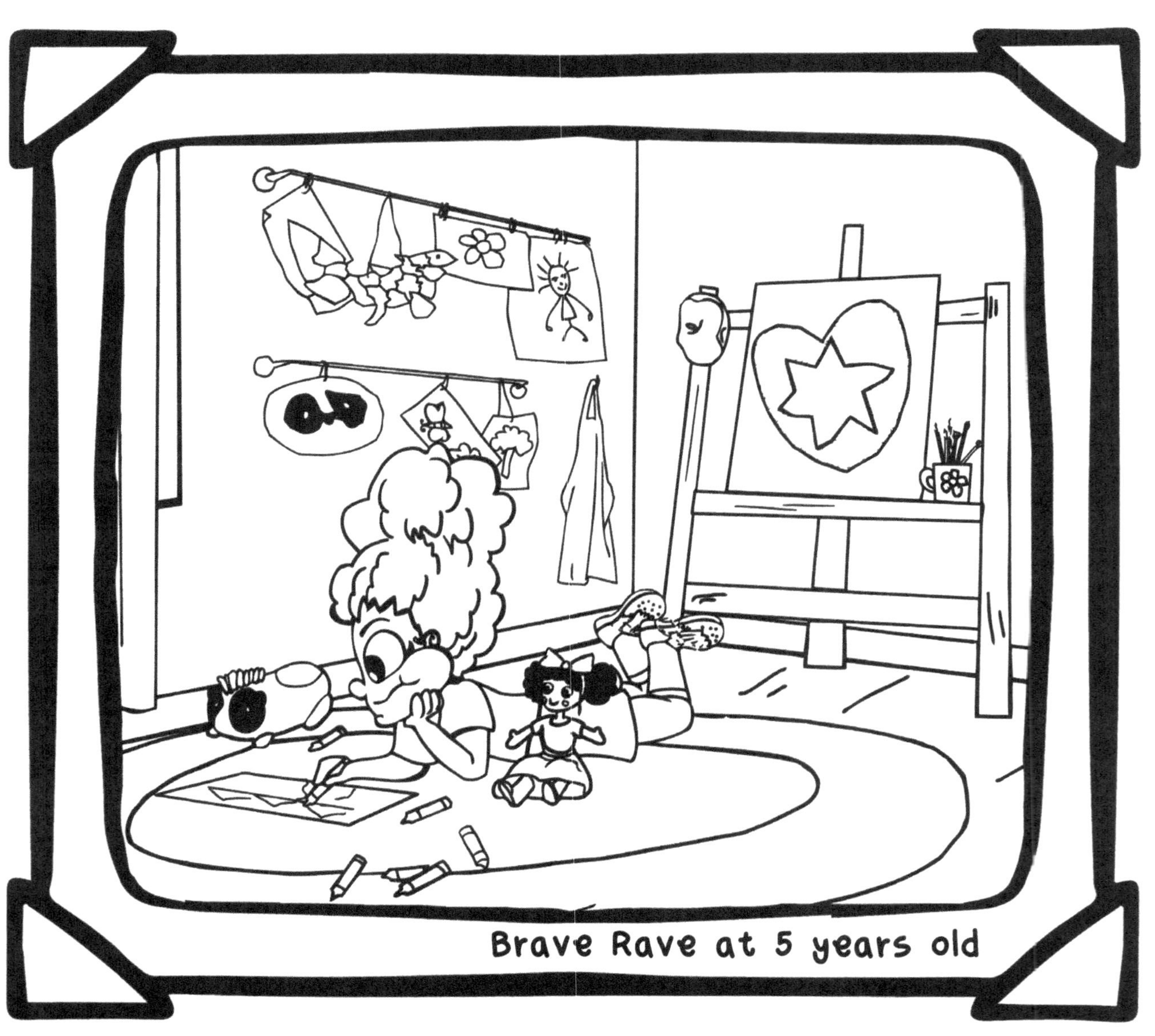

Brave Rave at 5 years old

IMAGINE

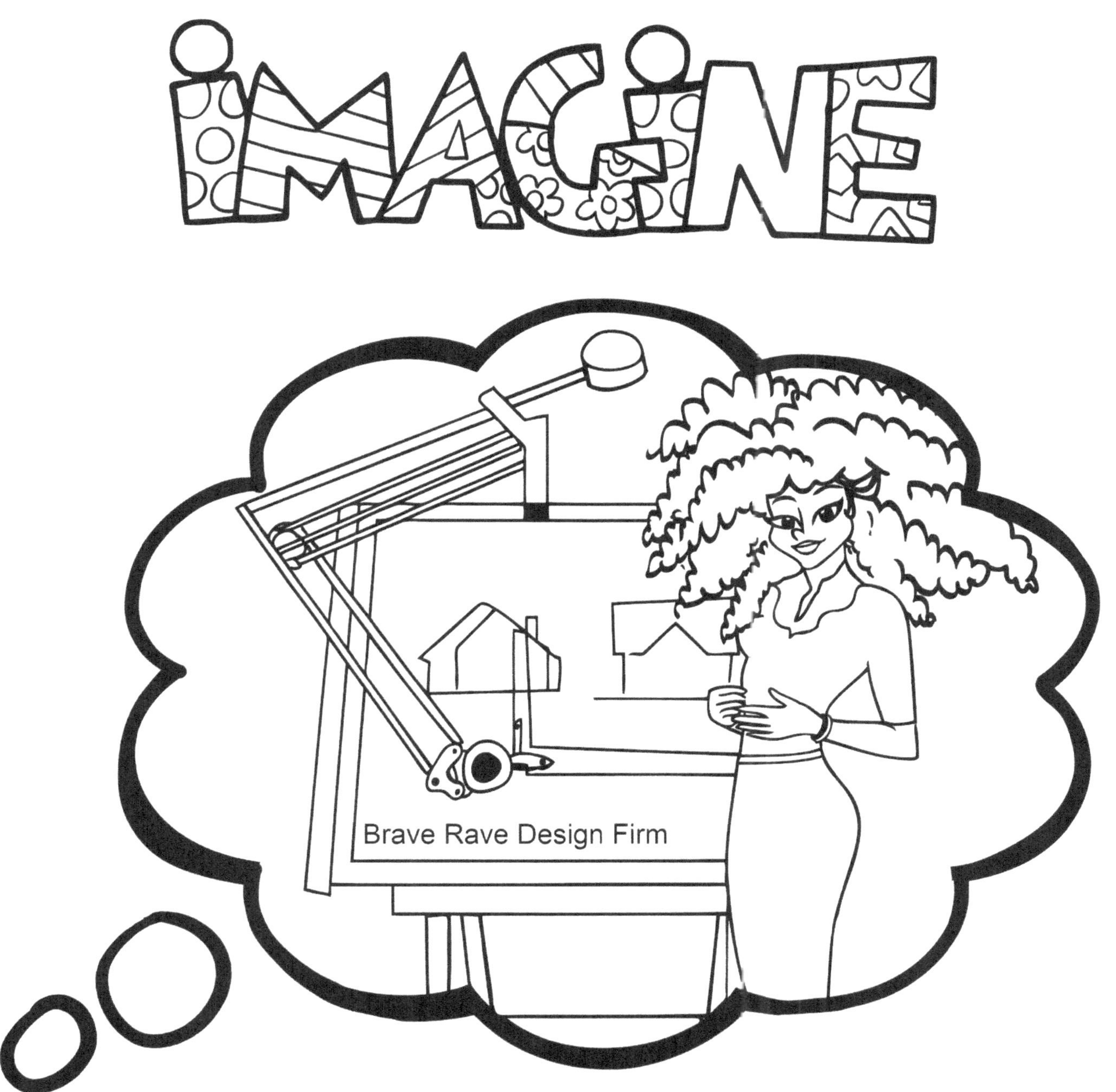

being an architect; using my drawing skills to design buildings, homes, neighborhoods, and cities.

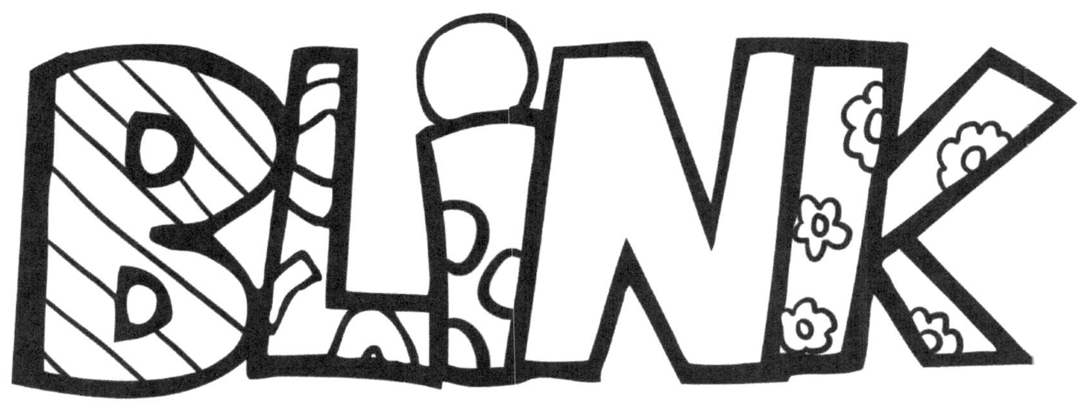
BLINK

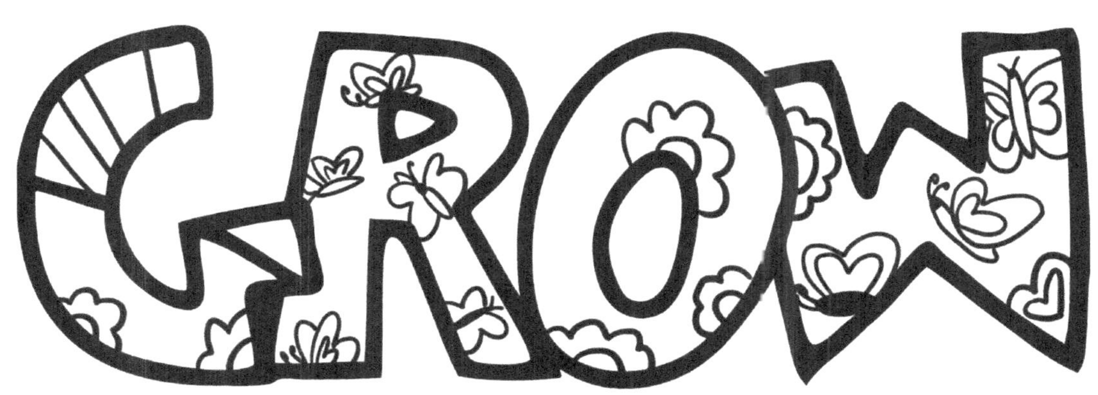
GROW

I put on my prettiest, most Feel-Good outfit for the day.

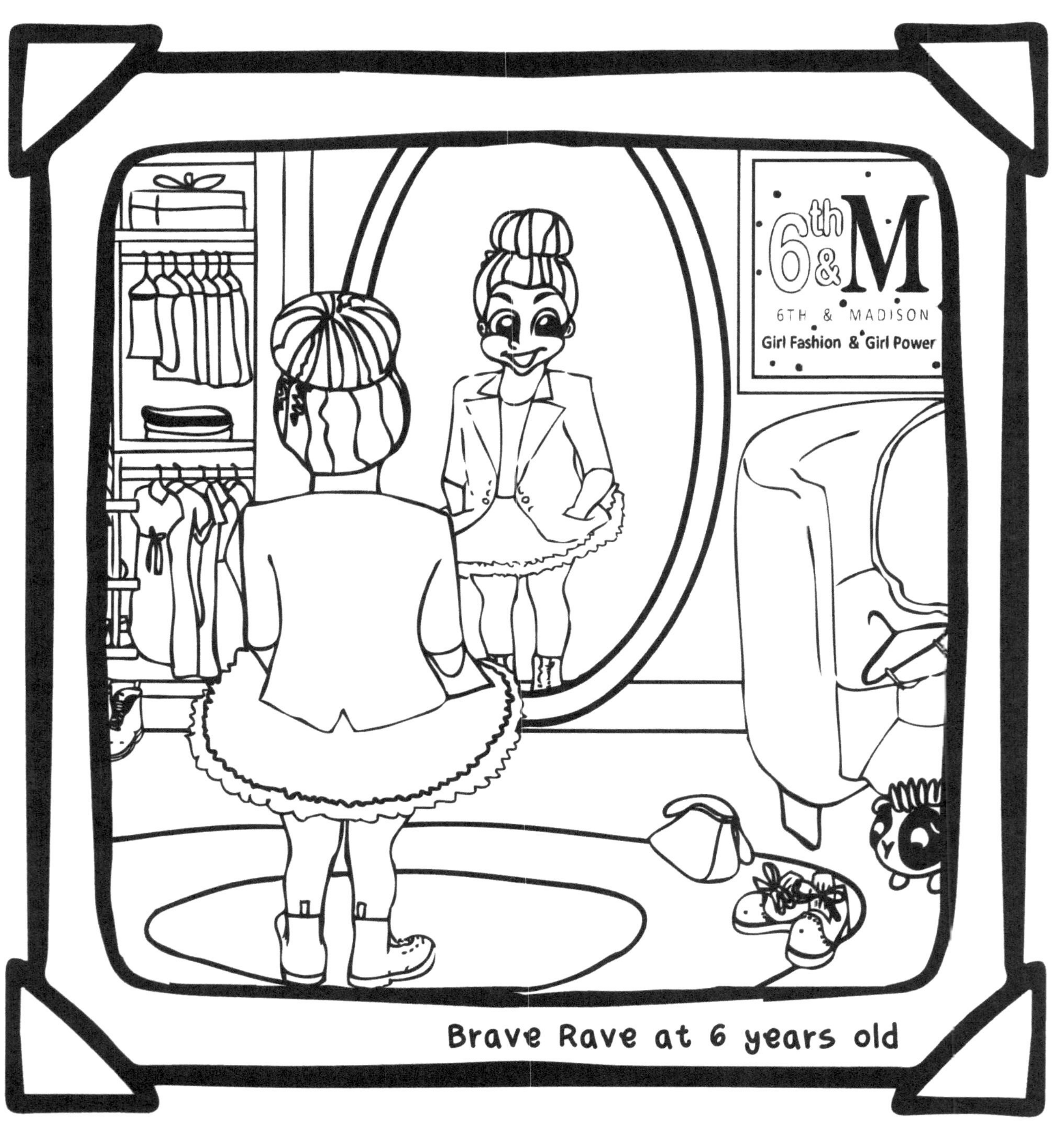

Brave Rave at 6 years old

IMAGINE

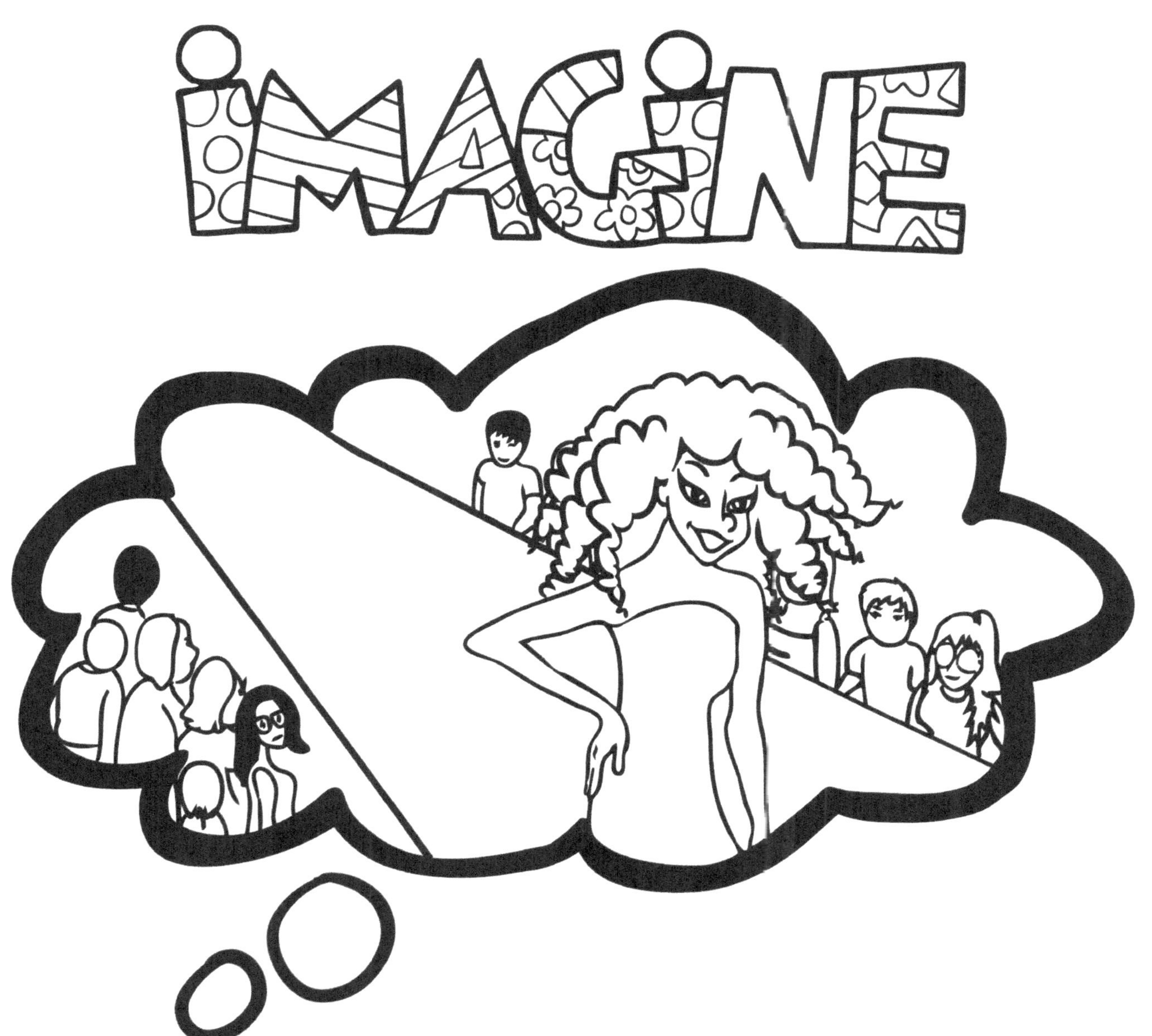

being a super model walking down runways or a fashion designer showing off my beautifully crafted designs to people from all over the world.

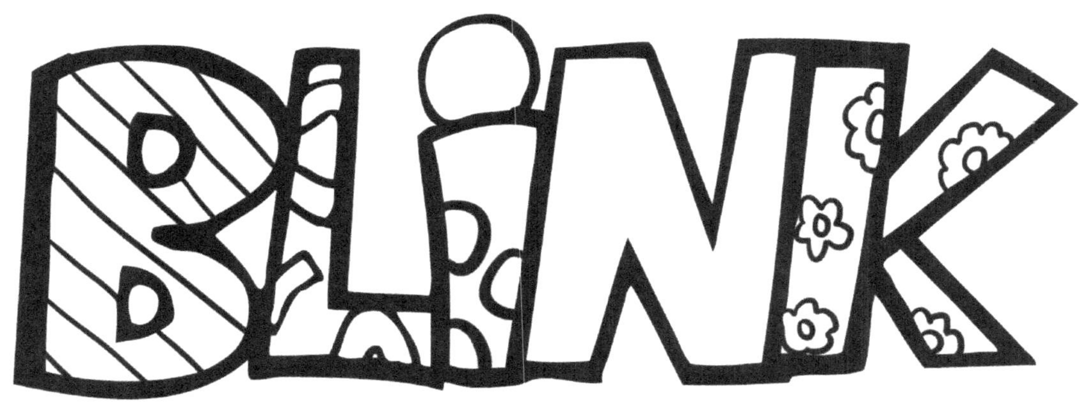
BLINK

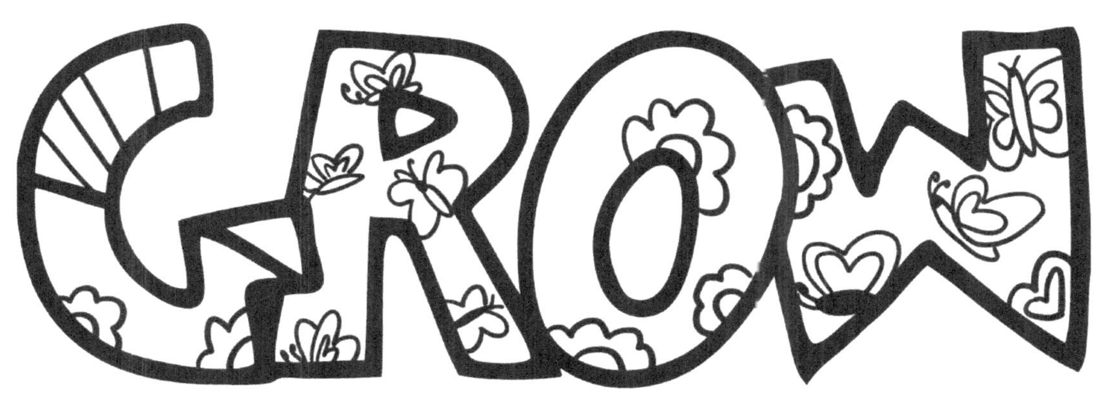
GROW

Dad is in the garden. I help him to dig-dig-dig in the dirt to plant fruits and vegetables that we will one day use to prepare healthy meals.

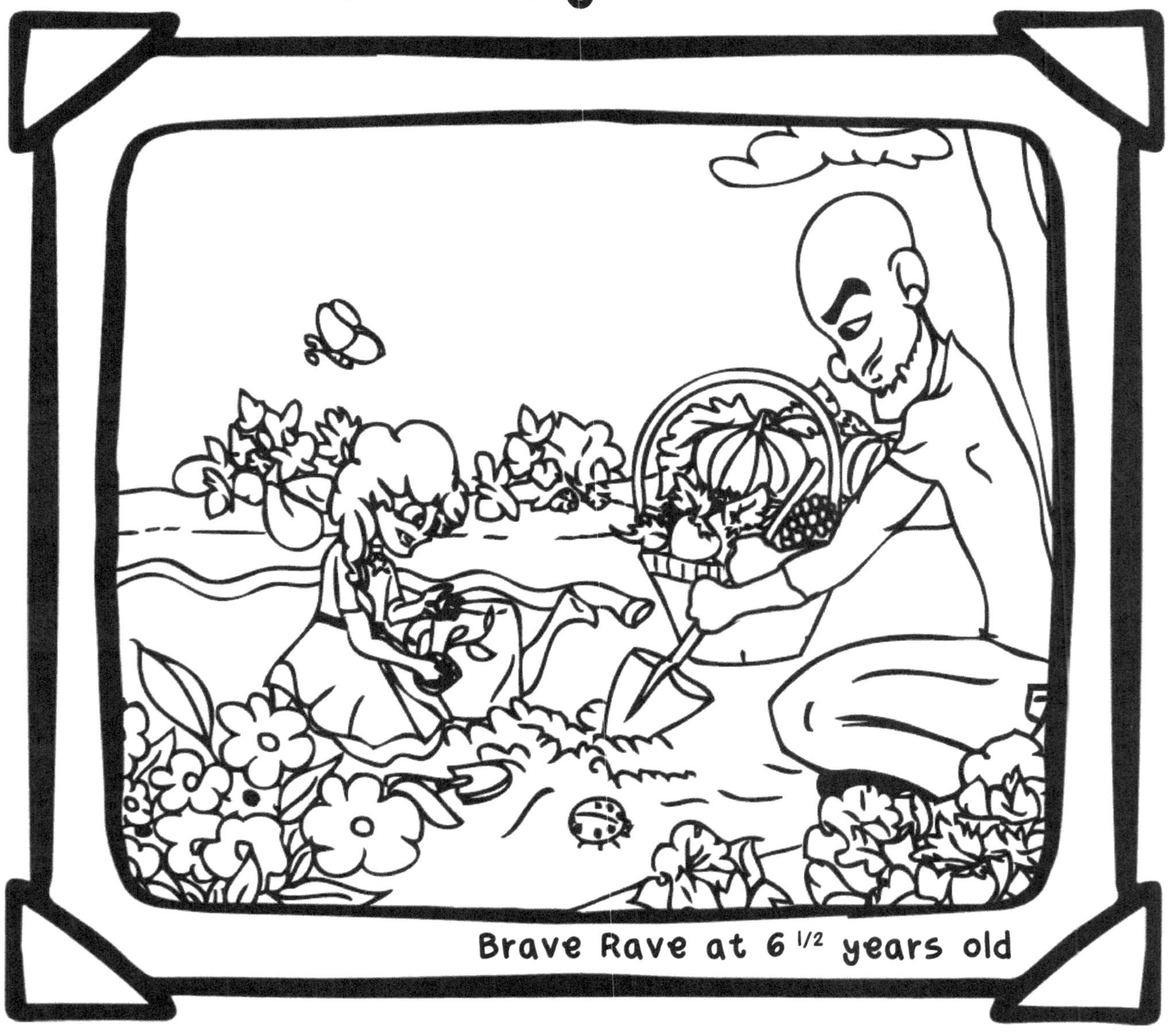

Brave Rave at 6 ½ years old

IMAGINE

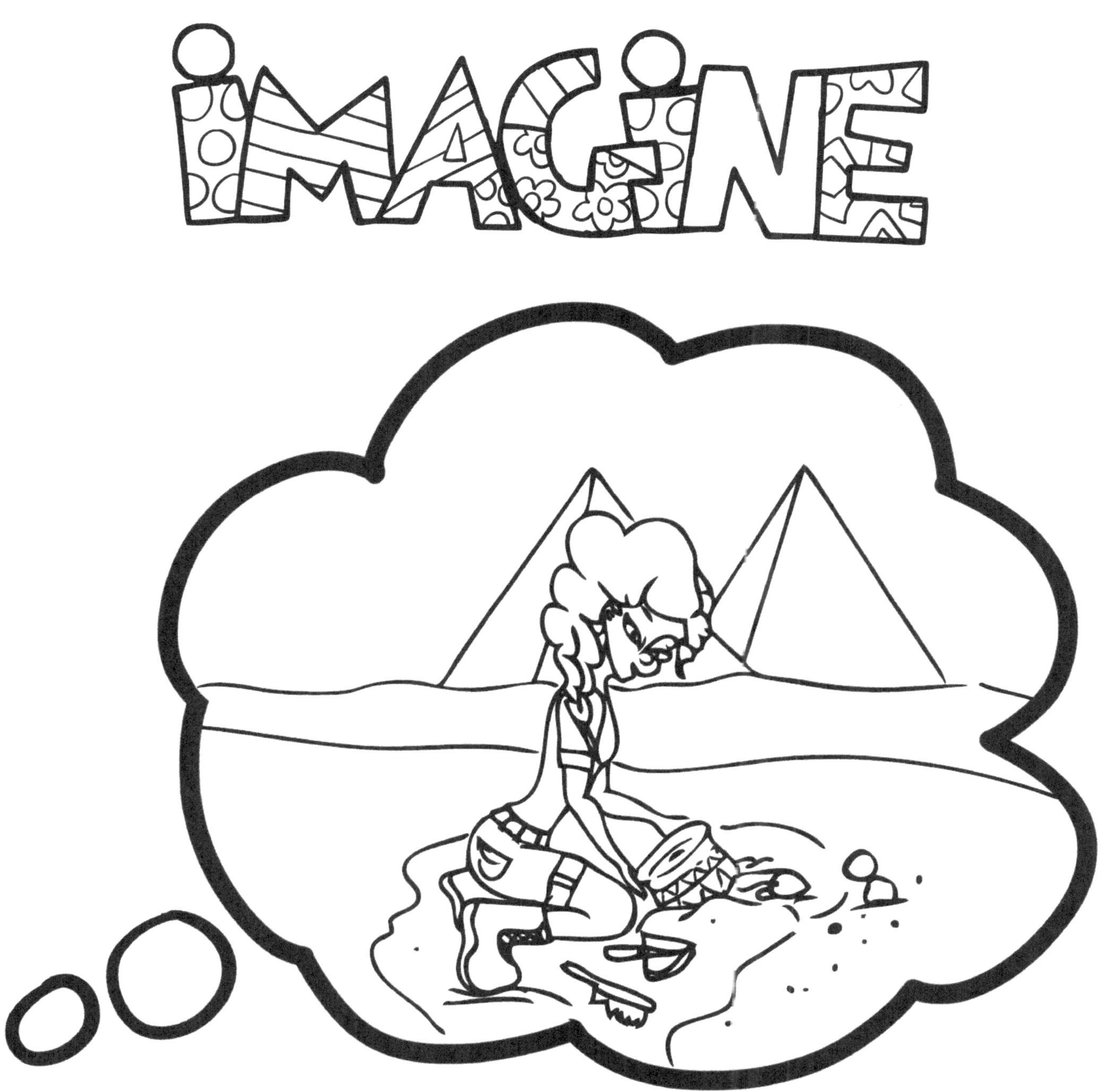

being an archeologist in Africa,
uncovering ancient artifacts
buried in the dirt and sand.

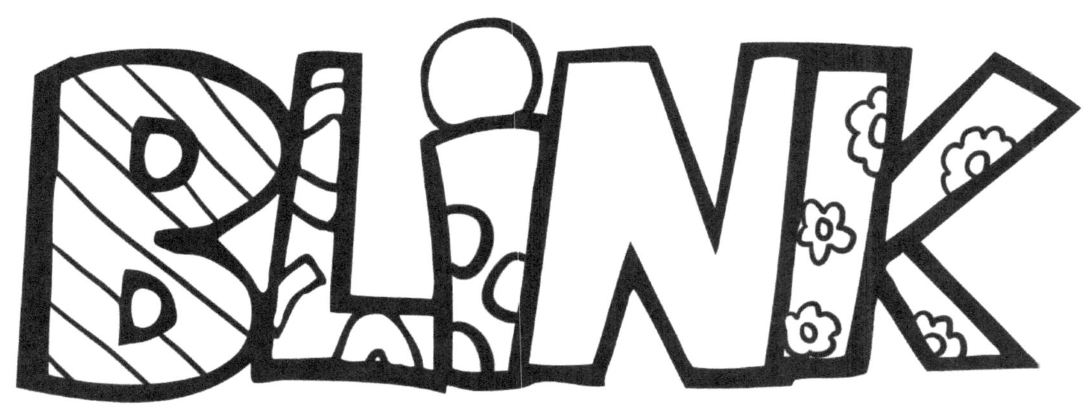

33

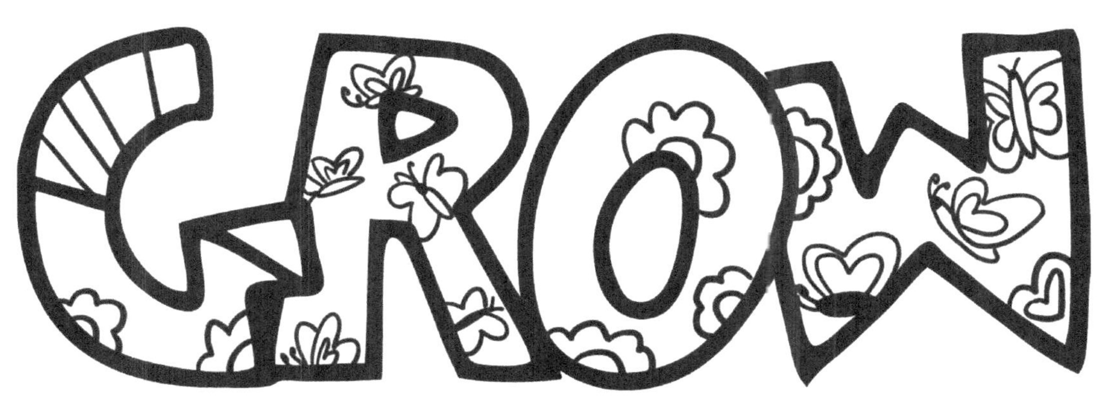
GROW

I help my parents prepare delicious meals made from fresh fruits and vegetables gathered from our garden to keep us energized and healthy.

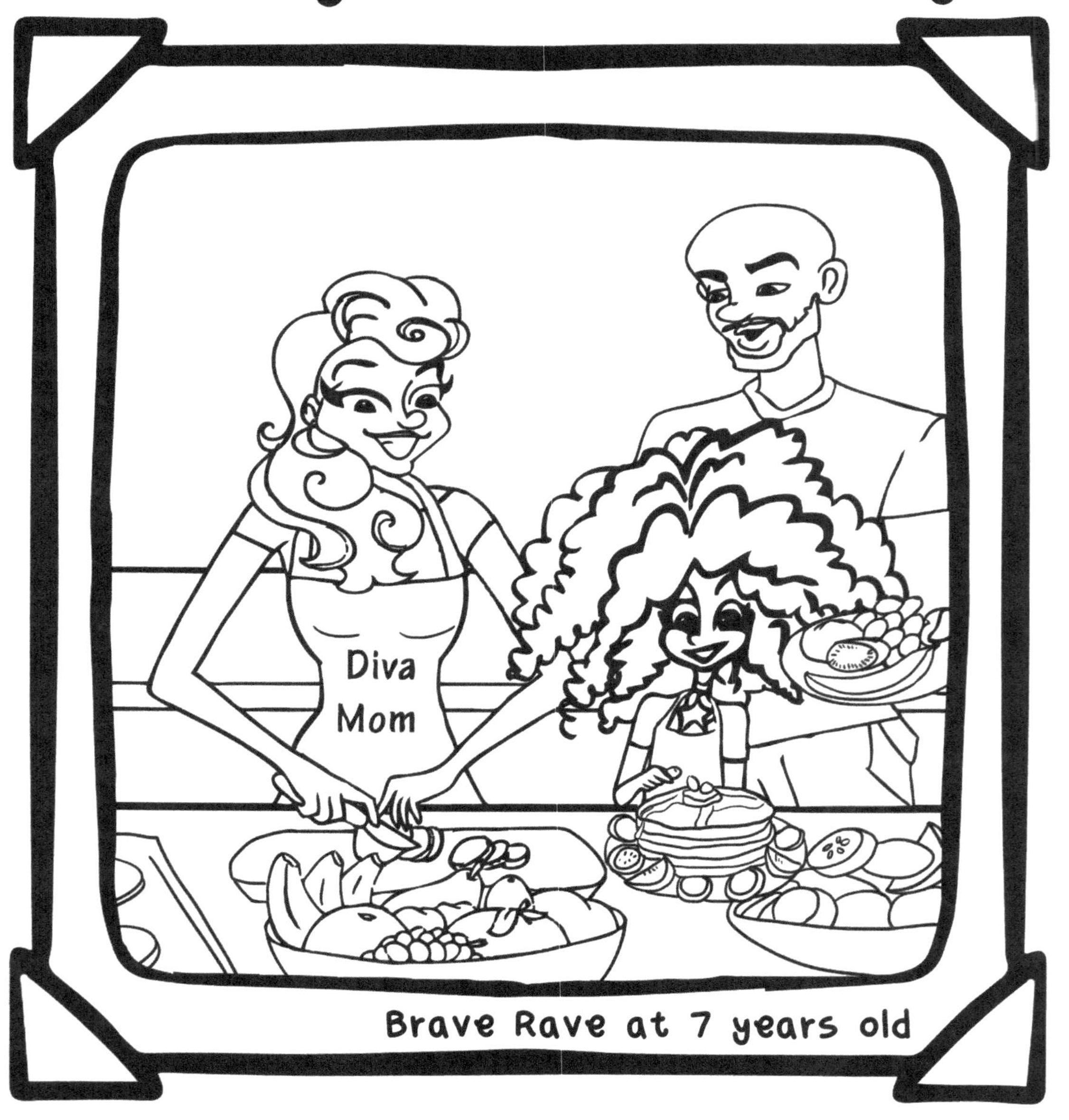

Brave Rave at 7 years old

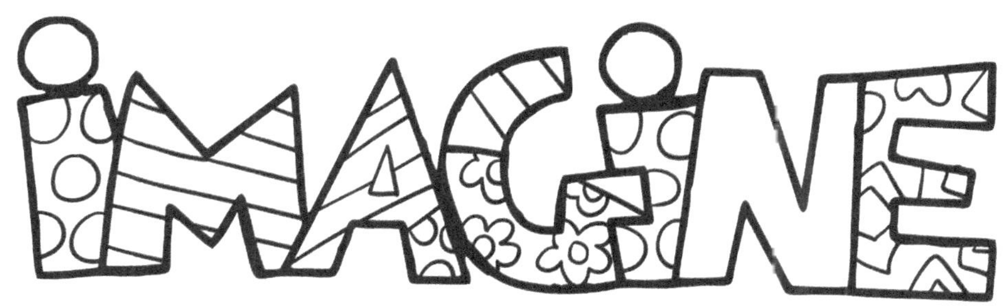

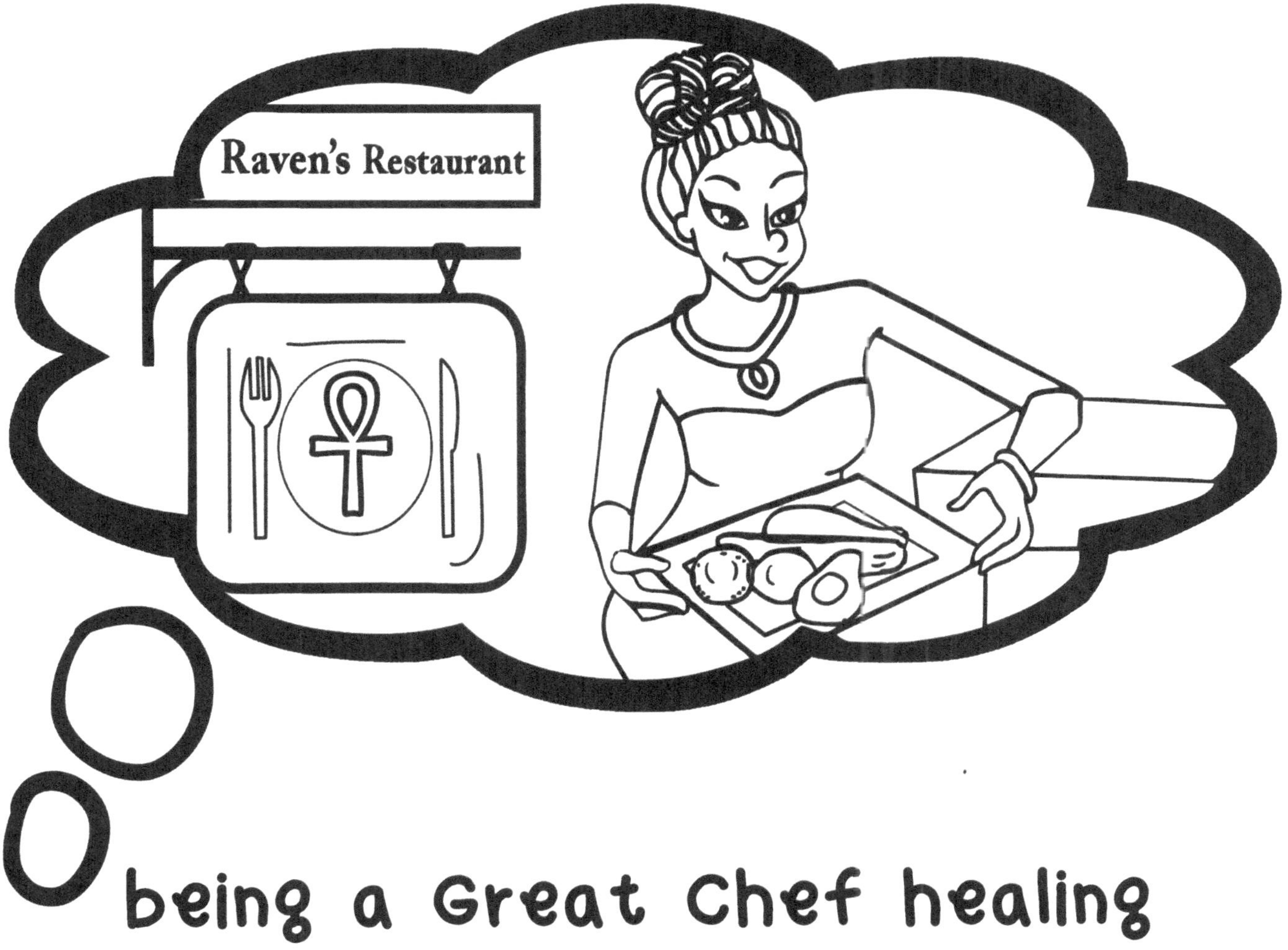

being a Great Chef healing people with healthy delicious magical fruits and vegetables from the Earth.

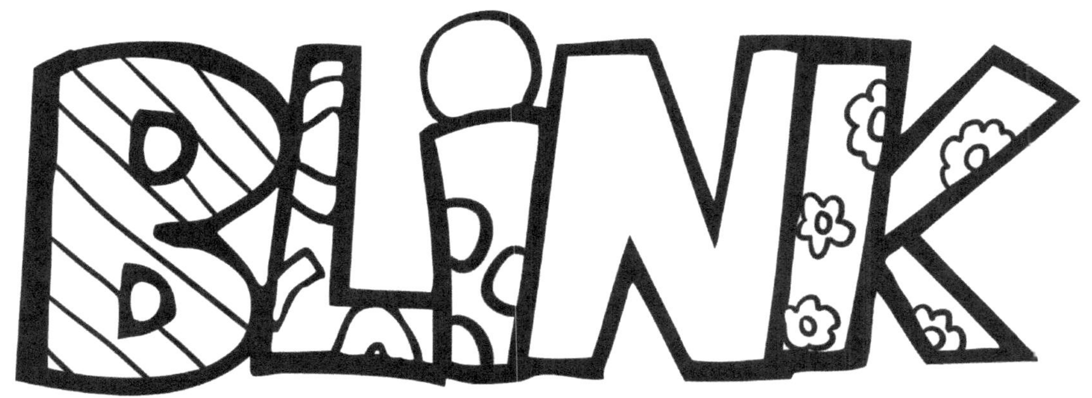
BLINK

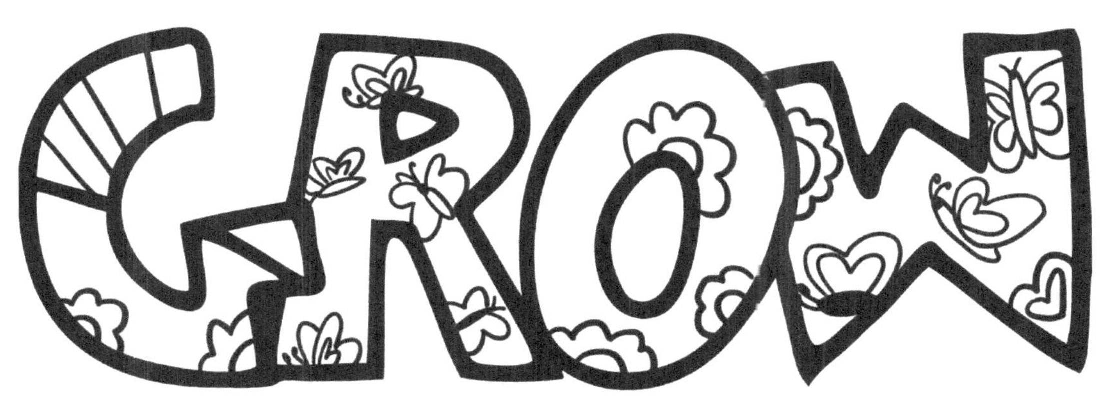
GROW

Mom does my hair to keep it healthy and growing. It makes me feel like Royalty. She says my hair is my true crown and to treat it with great care.

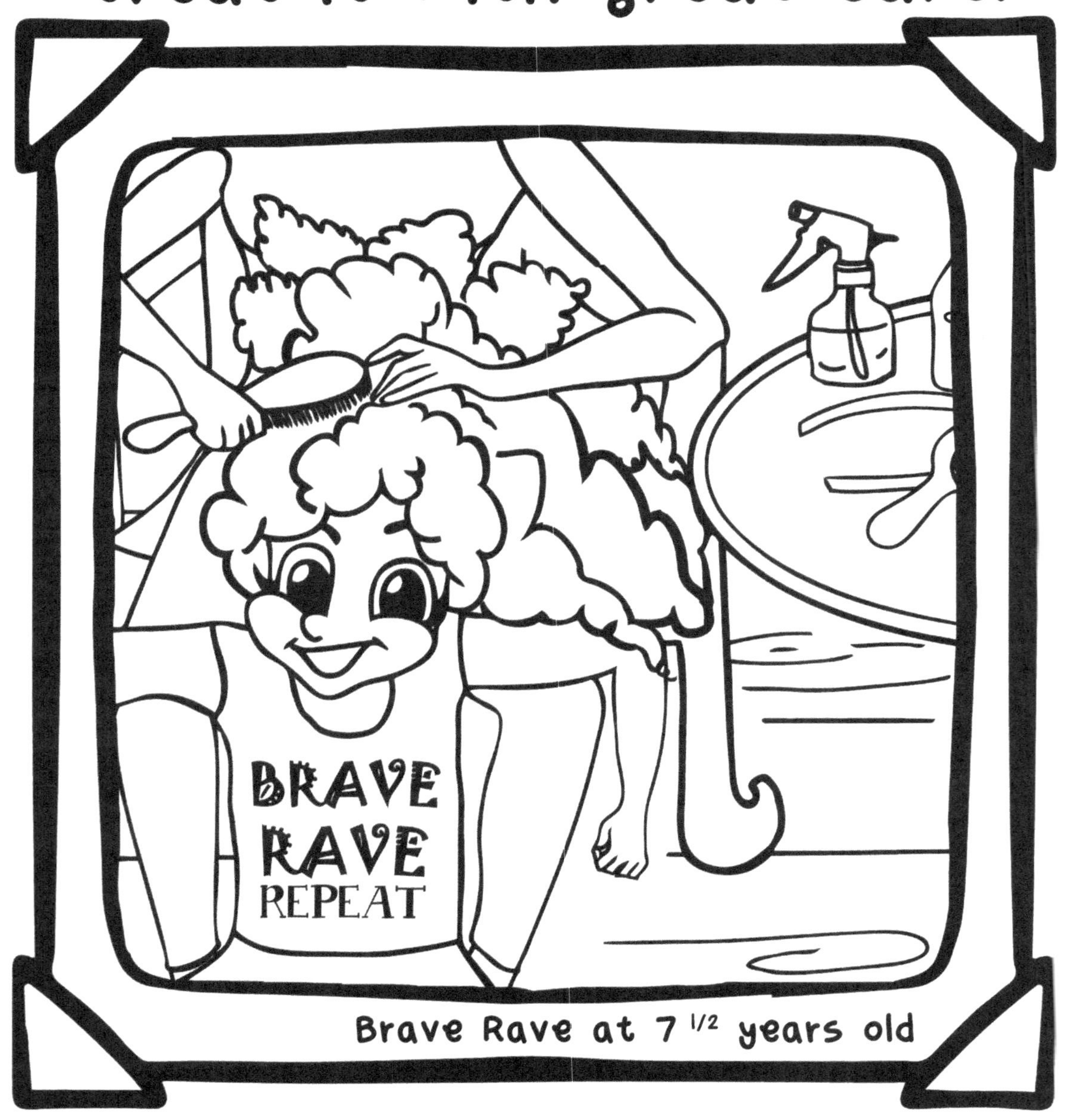

Brave Rave at 7 ½ years old

IMAGINE

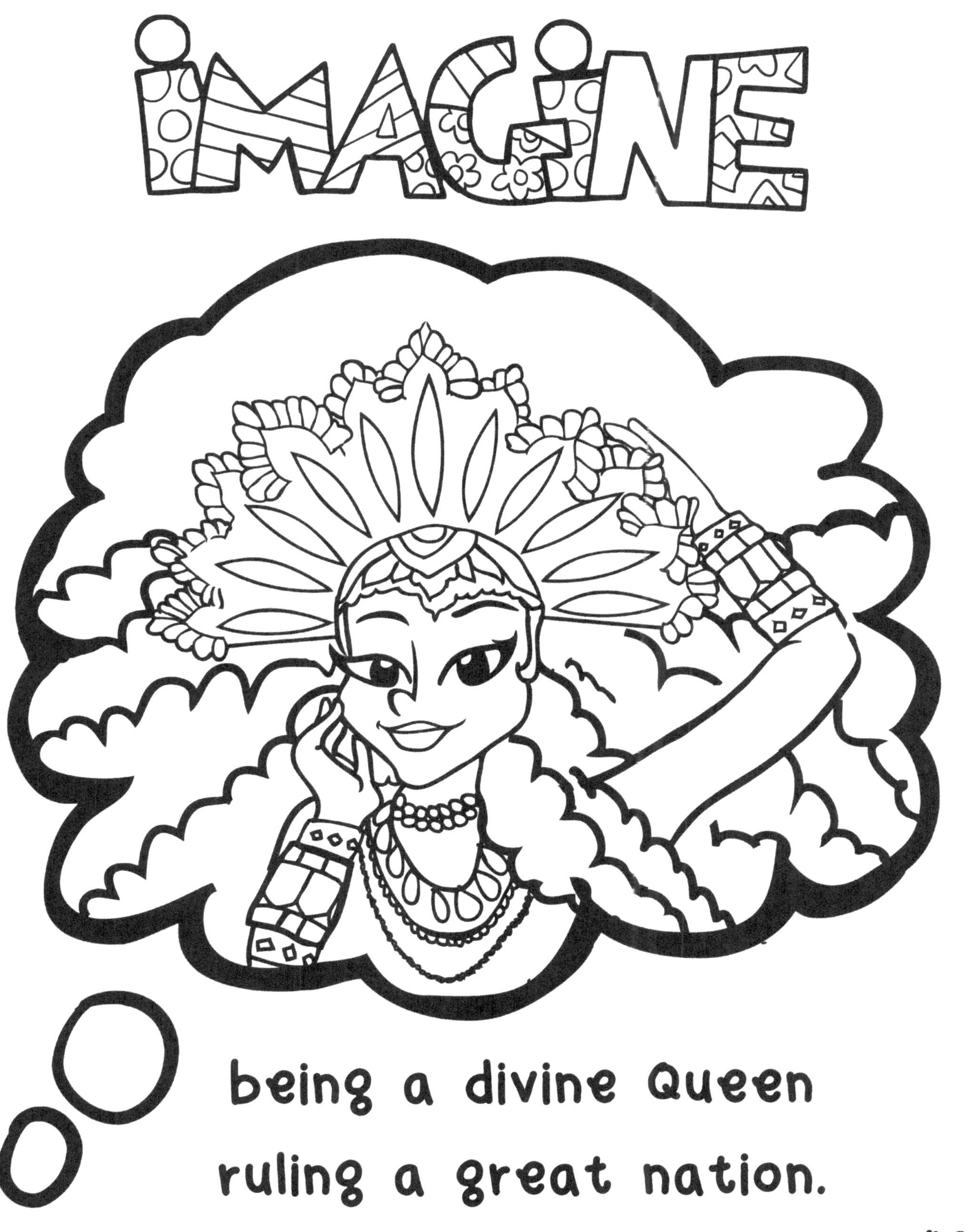

being a divine Queen
ruling a great nation.

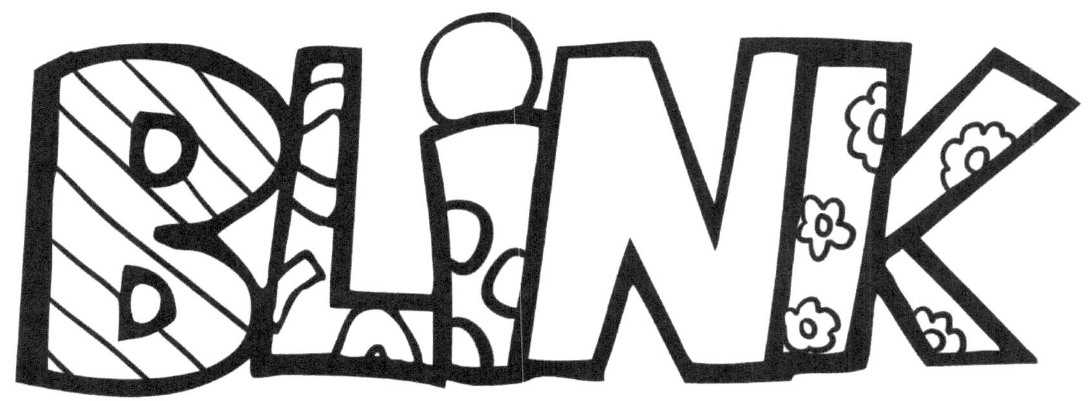

BLINK

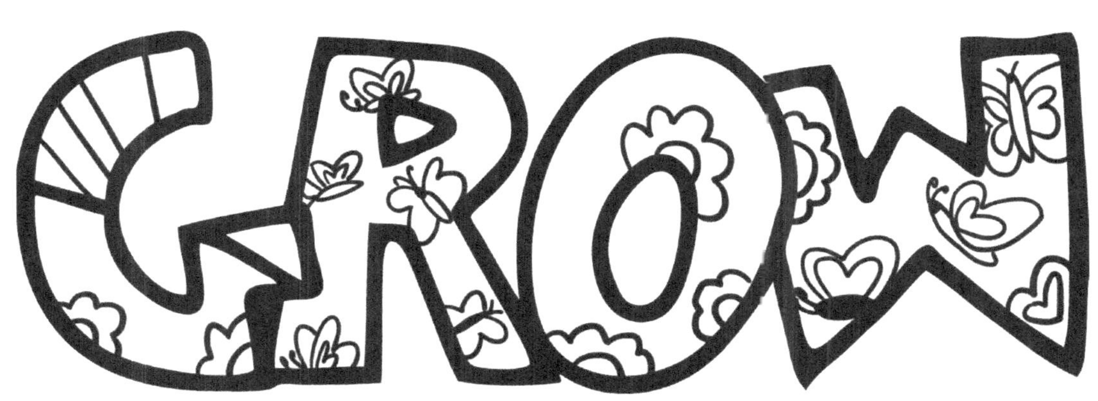
GROW

I always take time to practice my
Dance-Dance-Dance-Dance.
It keeps my body healthy.

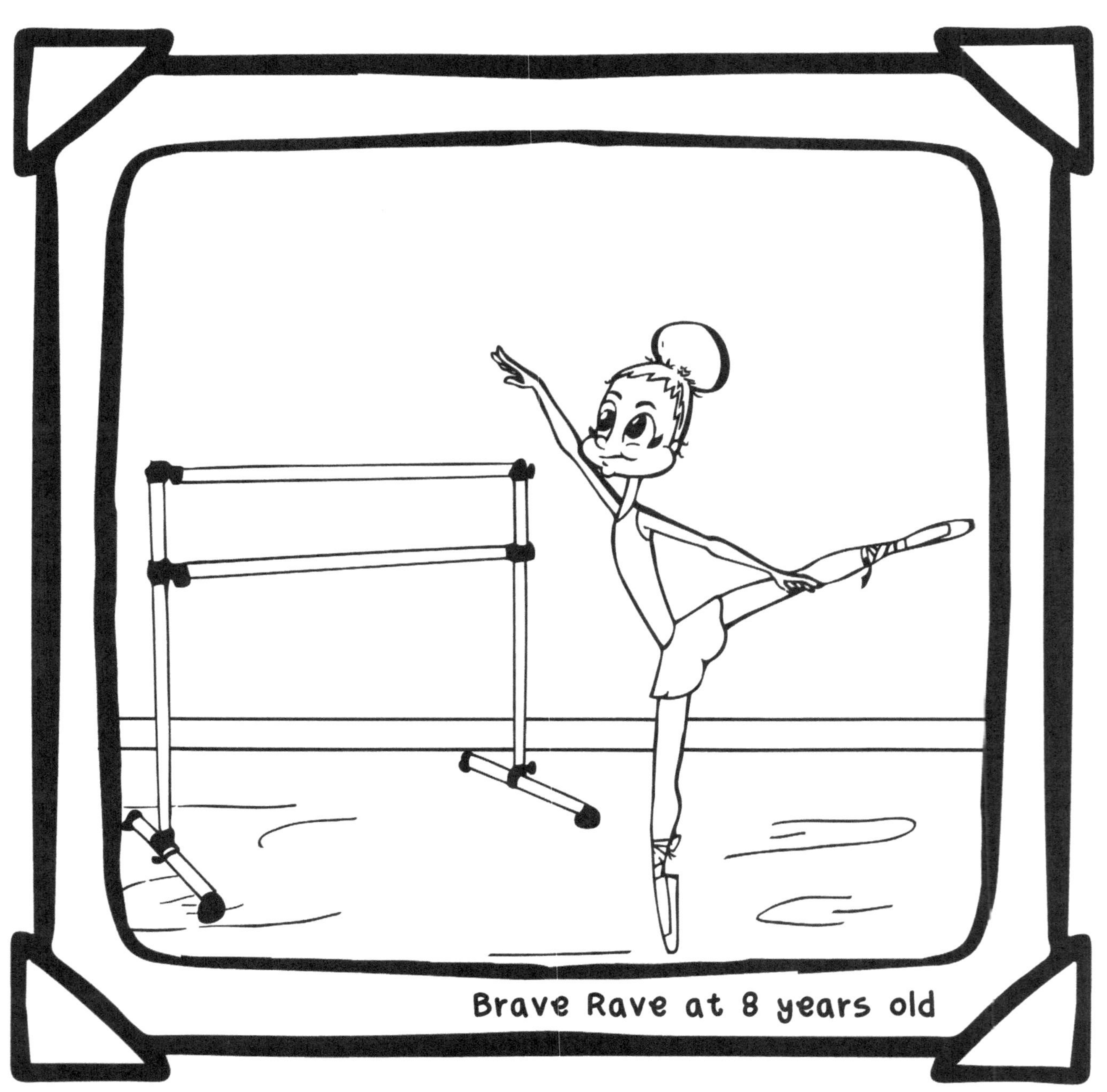

Brave Rave at 8 years old

IMAGINE

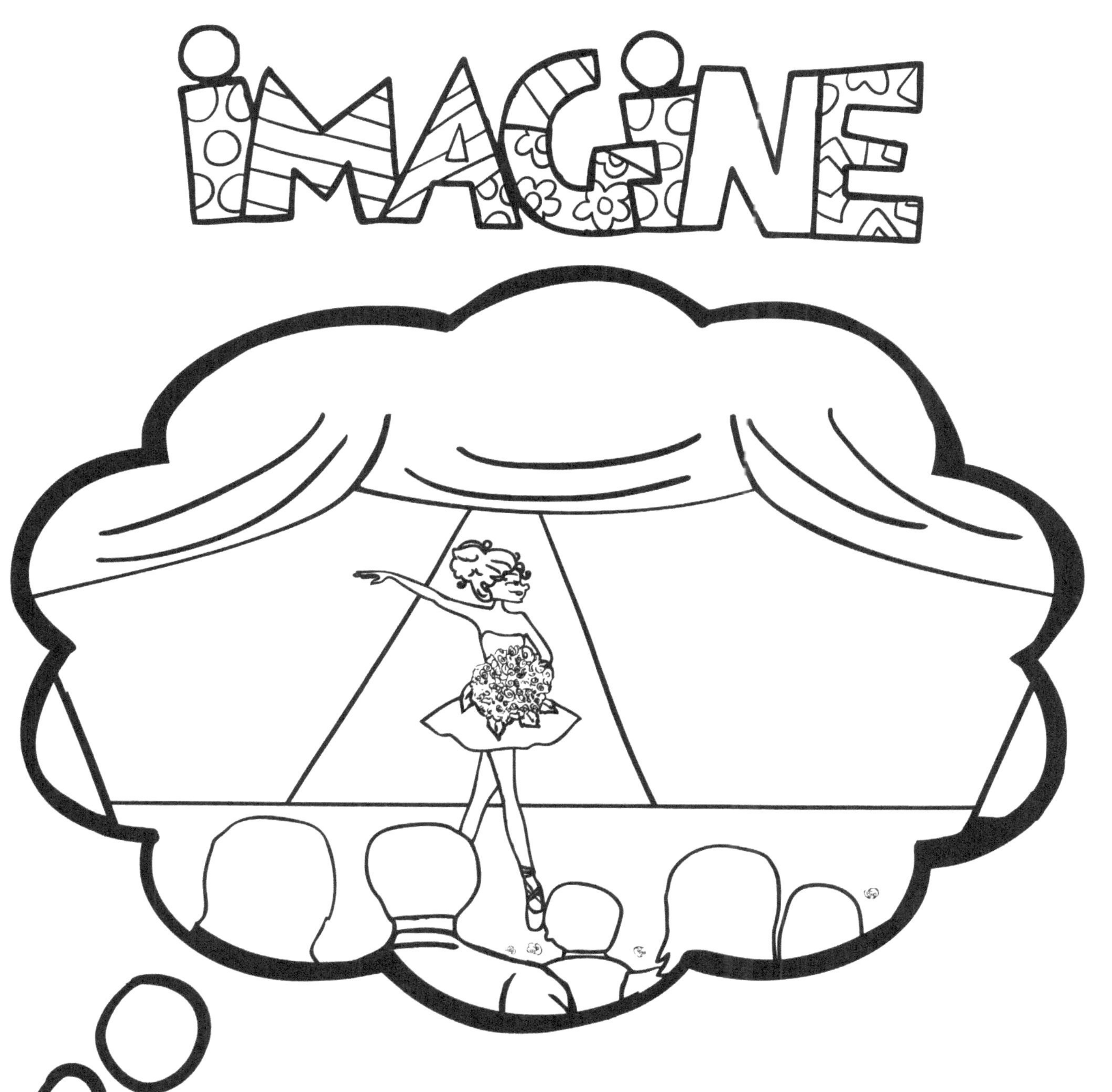

being the prima ballerina
performing at the ballet in
front of a huge audience.

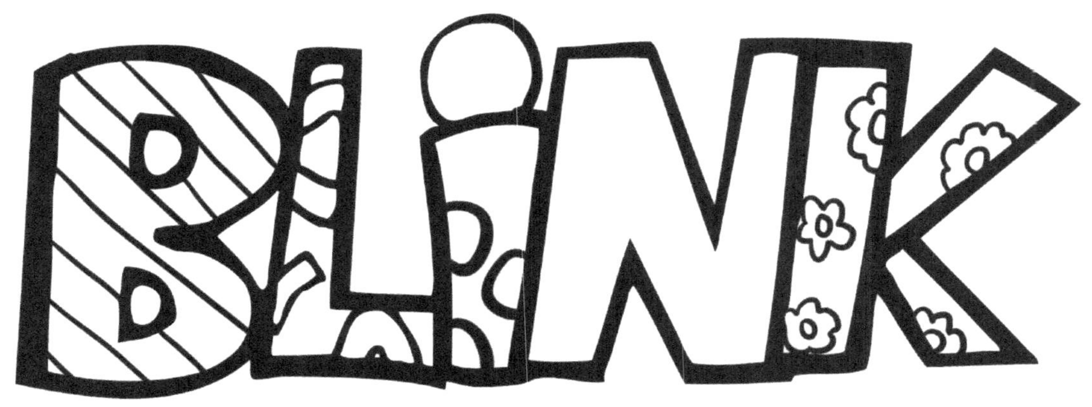
BLINK

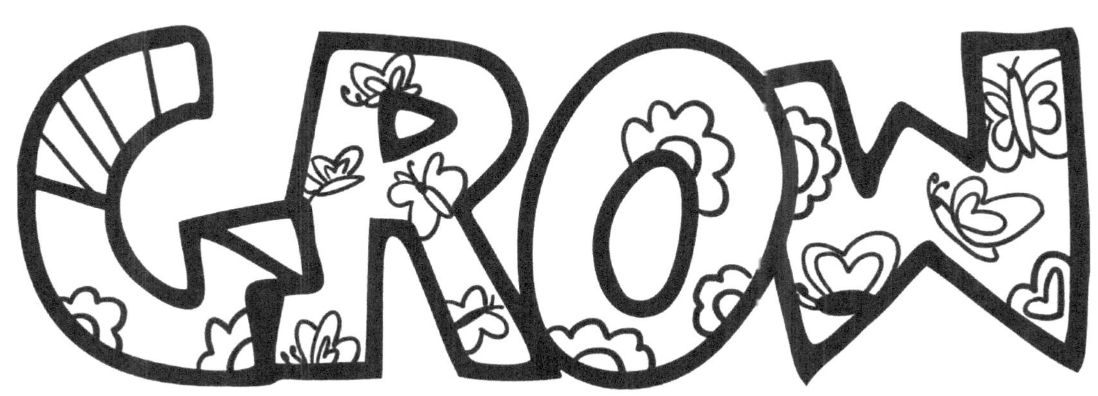
GROW

I write all of my day's thoughts,
feelings, and dreams in my diary.

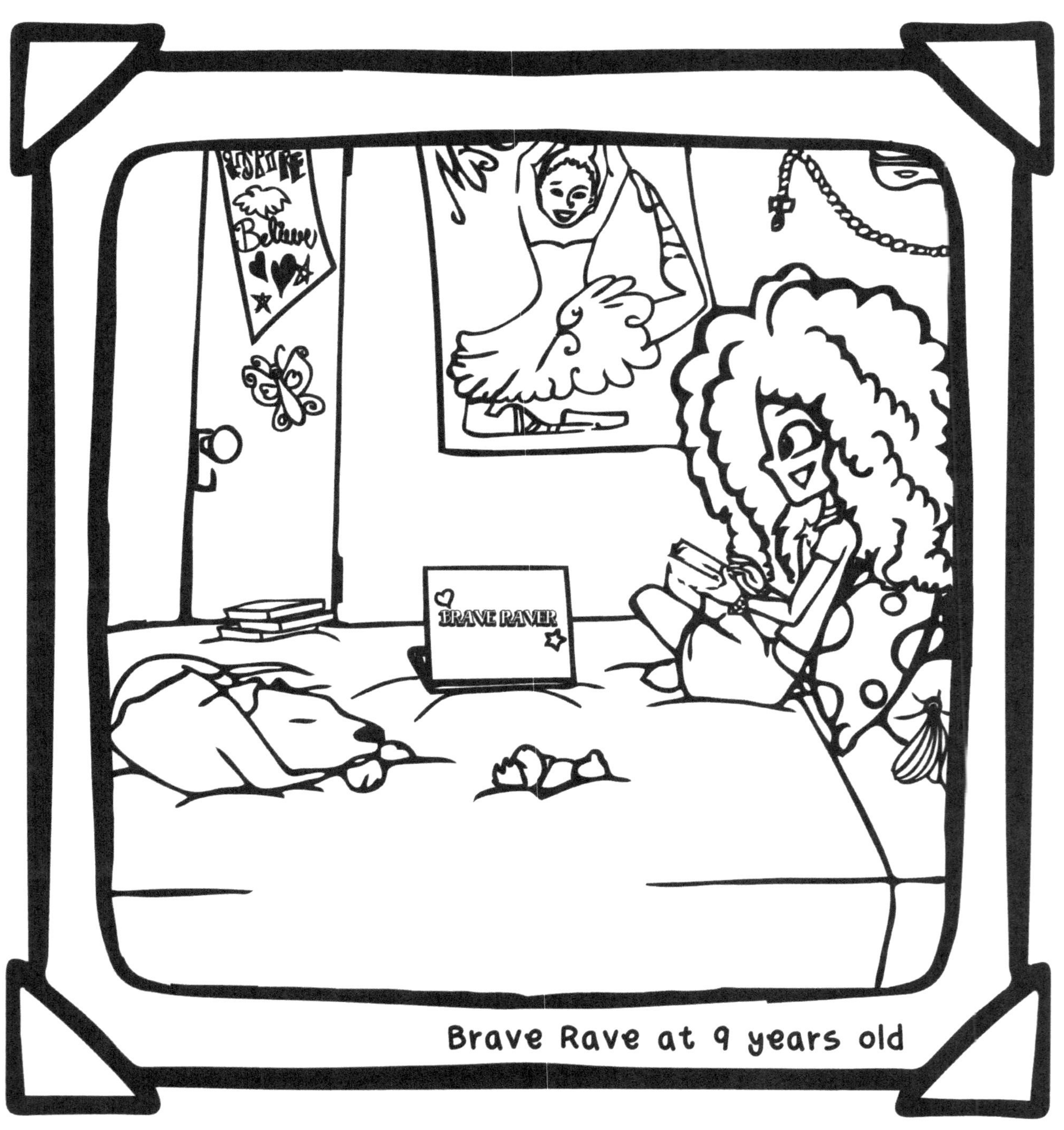

Brave Rave at 9 years old

IMAGINE

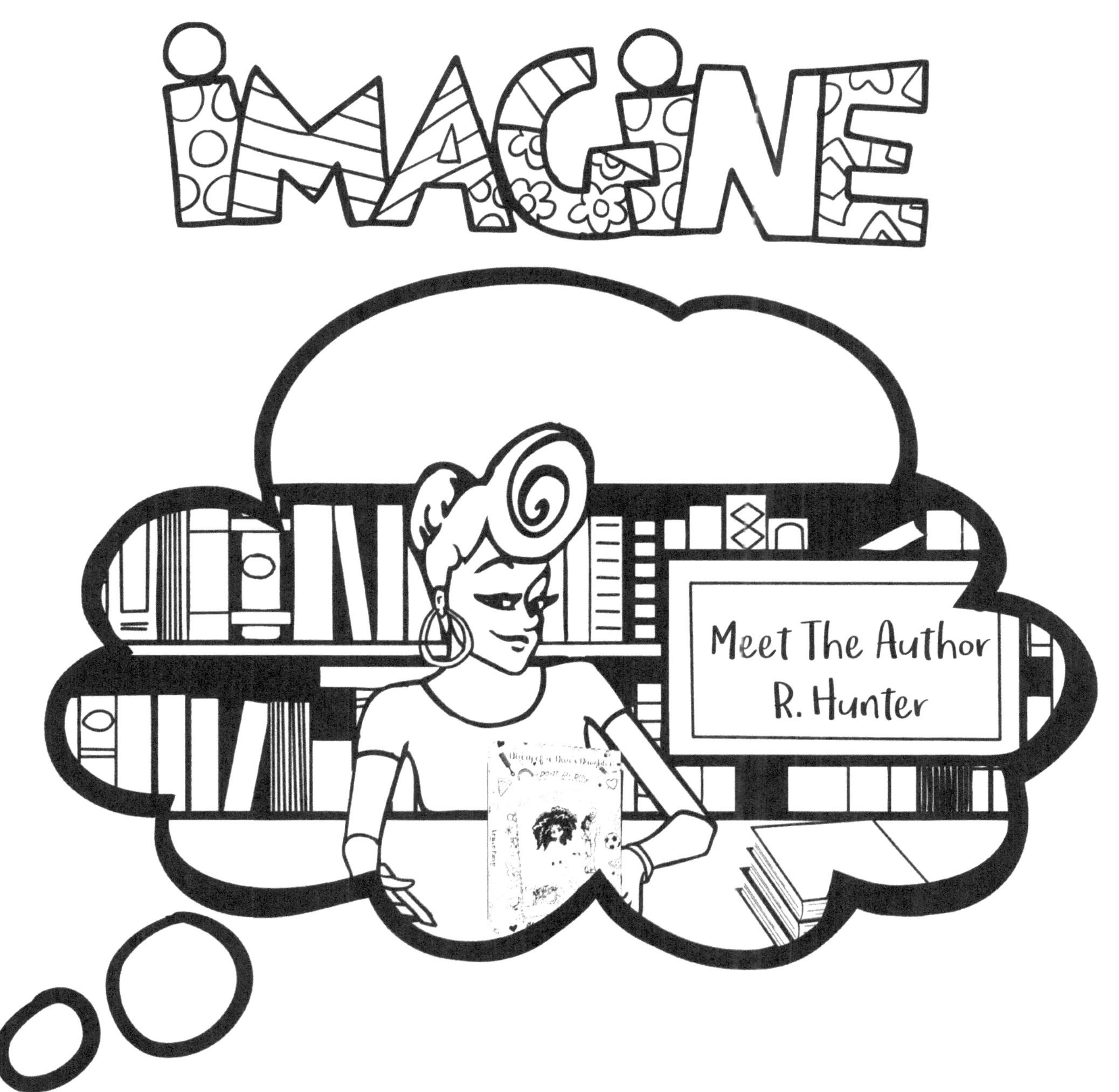

being a best selling author of books that share great stories that inspire the world.

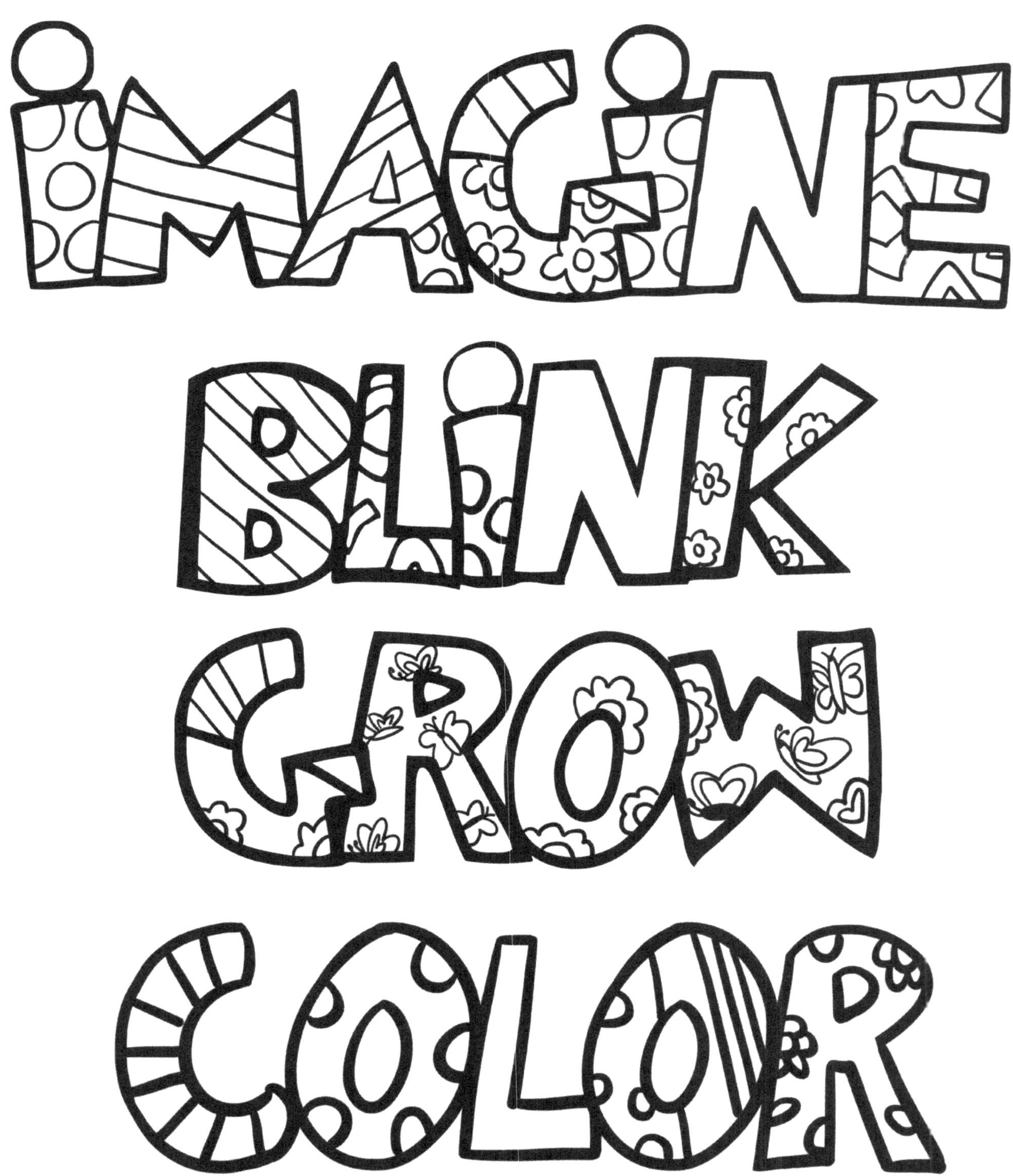

IMAGINE
BLINK
GROW
COLOR

to be Smart,
Kind, Brave,
and Beautiful
YOU.

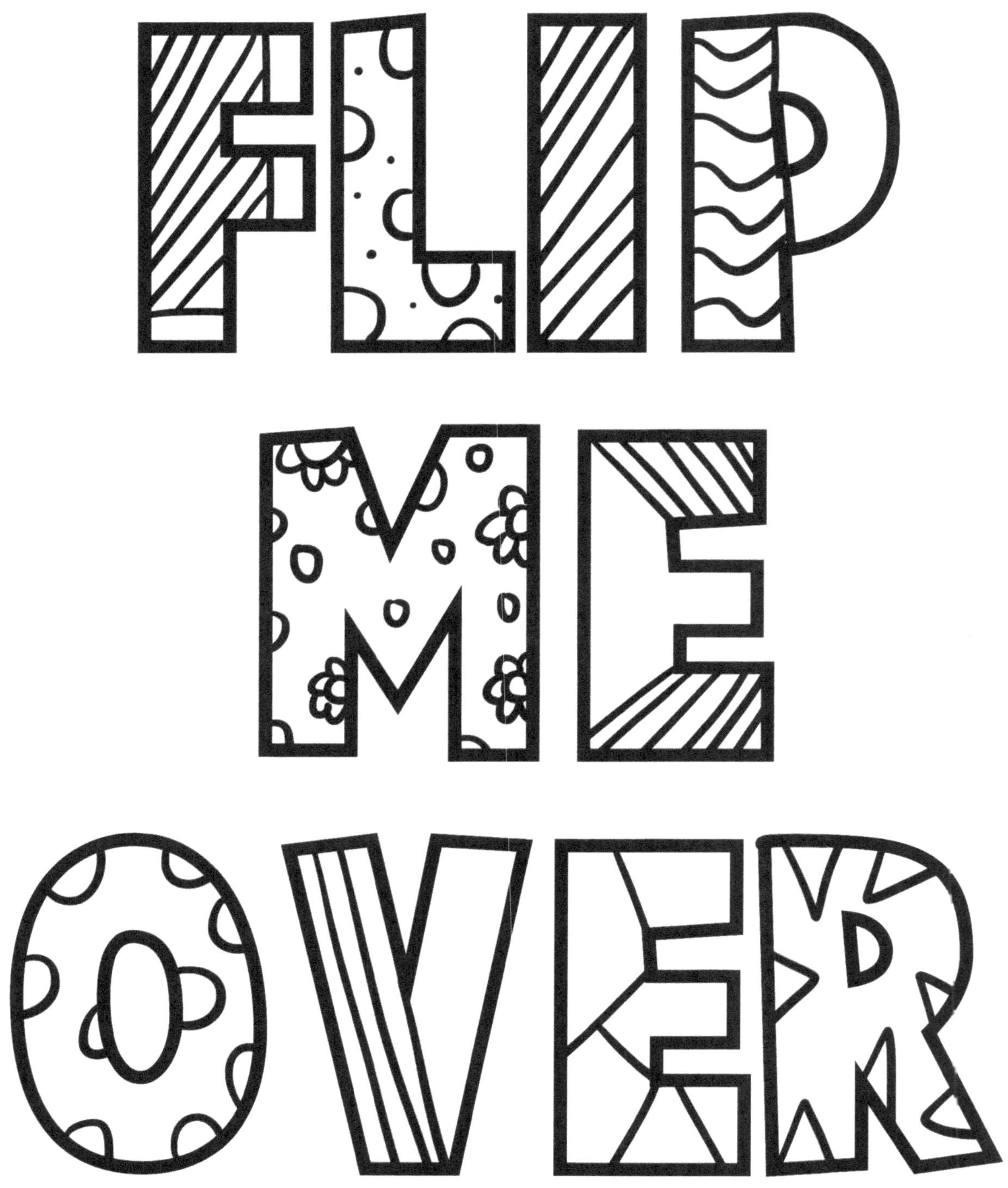

FLIP
ME
OVER

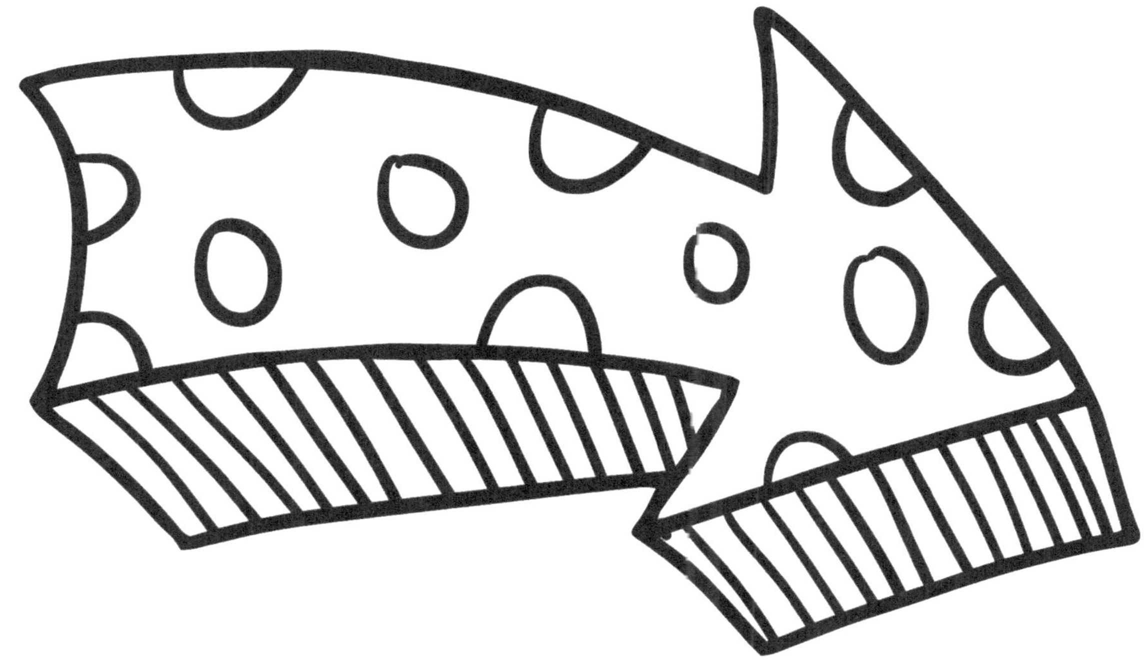

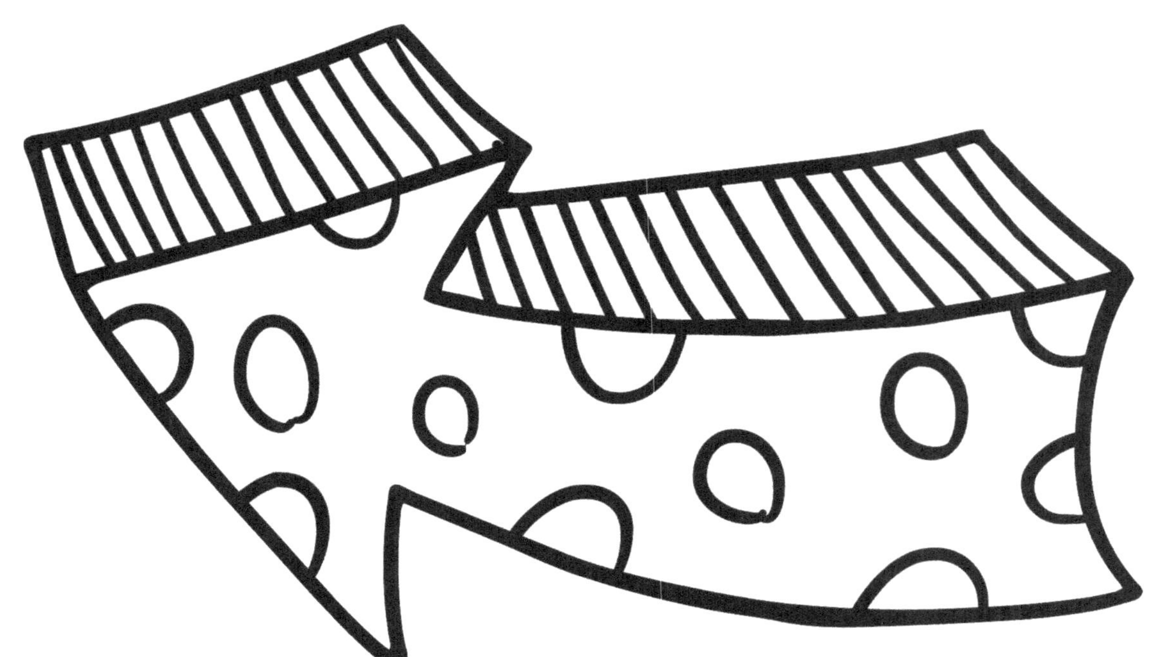

Diary of Brave Rave (Baby) - Writing Book

978-0-9973598-9-3

❋ Flower Press LLC
St. Louis, MO
BraveRaveBook.com

Thank you

to all the people who have been part
of this amazing experience–the good, the bad and the ALL. I want to
give a special thanks to my friends, family, teachers and mentors who
continued to encourage me to Image and Grow through this journey.

May we all
IMAGINE & GROW

The world is ours.
Take a Moment to Give back.

Diary of Baby Brave Rave

Writing Book

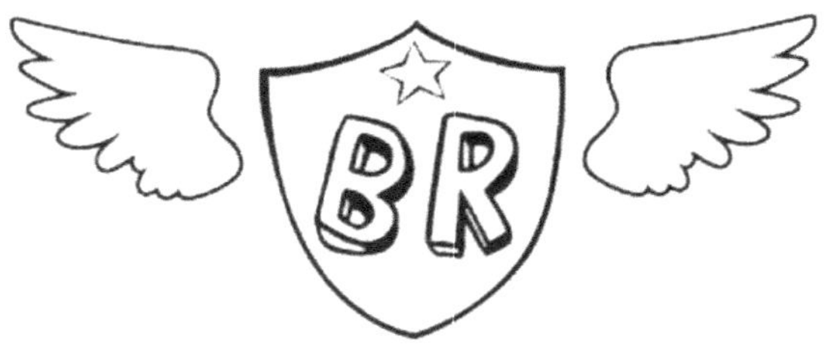

by Raquel Hunter

Flower Press Publishing

ABOUT THE AUTHOR

Raquel Hunter is a real-life **Diva Mom**, so she is perfectly qualified to write the **BRAVERAVE** book series. In fact, she's been seen writing this book wearing the cutest pink yoga pants and flip-flops that have more bling than the Queen of England's tiara.

More than anything else in the world, Raquel believes that little girls can grow up to do amazing things. After all, she joined the Navy when she was 17 years old and got to live in Japan during her four-year tour of duty. After that, she got a degree in social work and became a youth mentor. She has also designed purses and made candles.

These days, when she is not writing Brave Rave books or teaching yoga she is doing her most important job — being Raven's mom.

Raquel lives in St. Louis with her diva-in- training-daughter Raven and her husband, the **DO-IT-ALL DAD**.

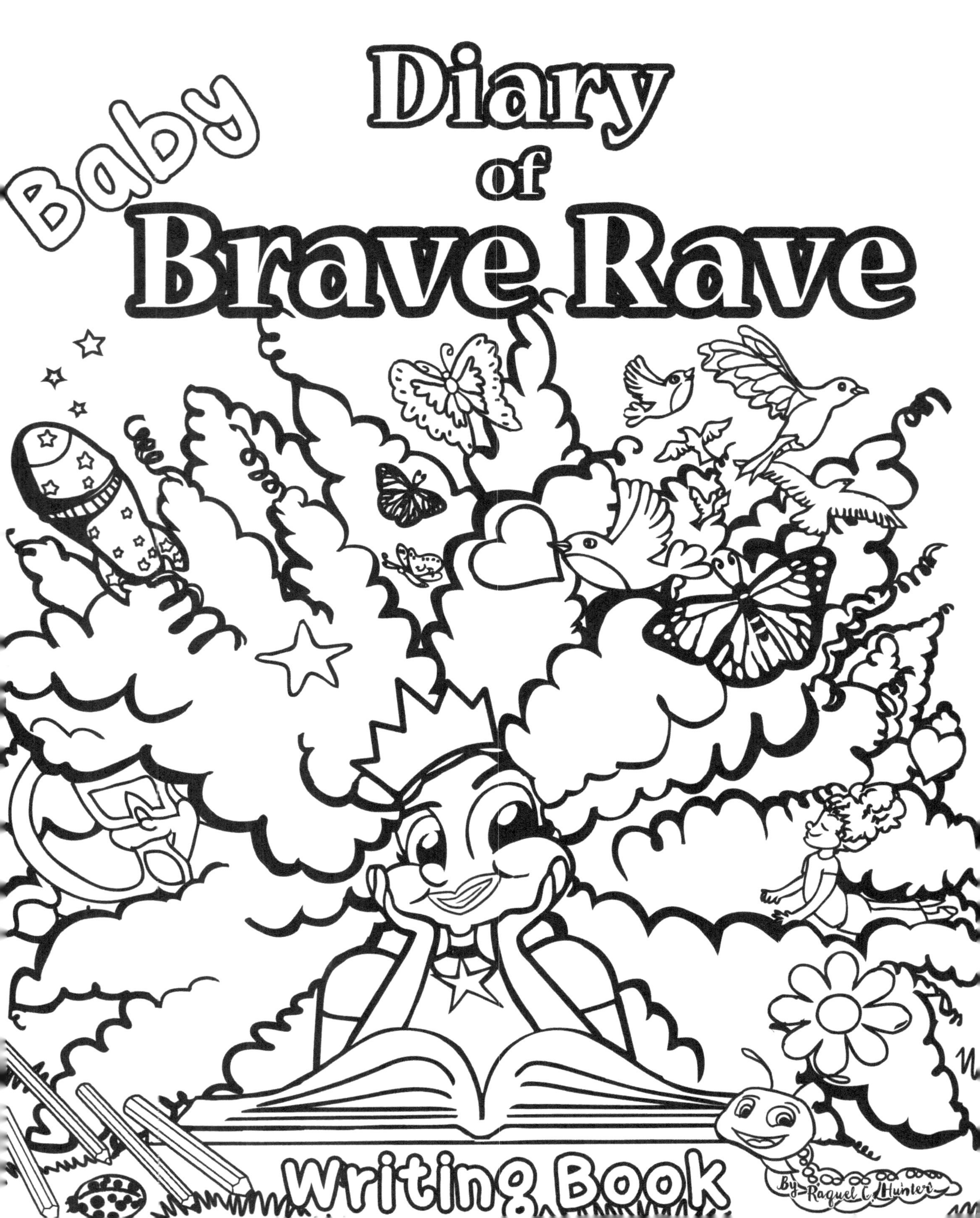

Baby
Diary
of
Brave Rave
Writing Book
By Raquel C. Hunter

Mom & Dad are always saying that I grow soooooo fast.

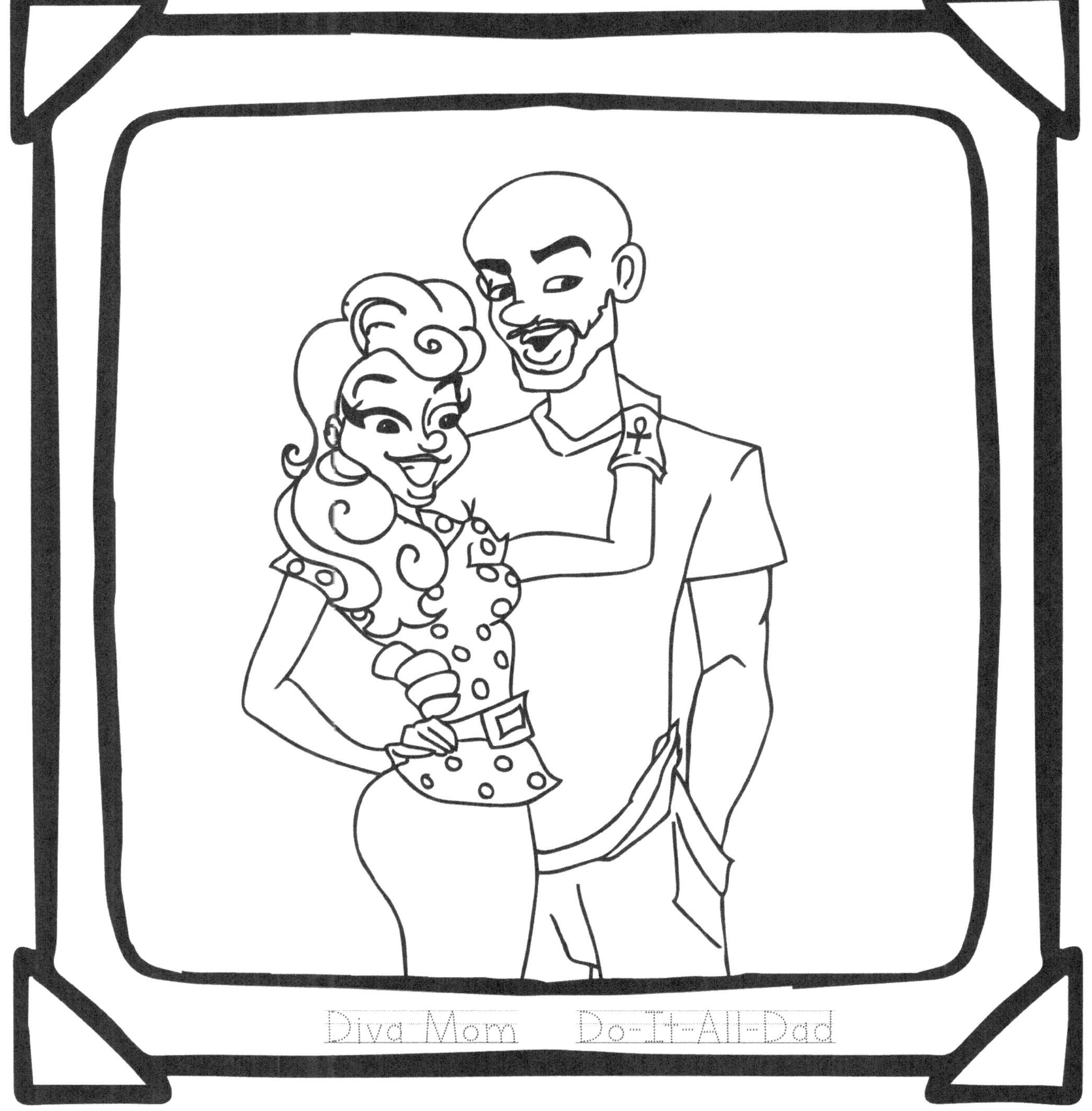

They say every time
they BLINK, I GROW.

Brave Rave
at 3 years old

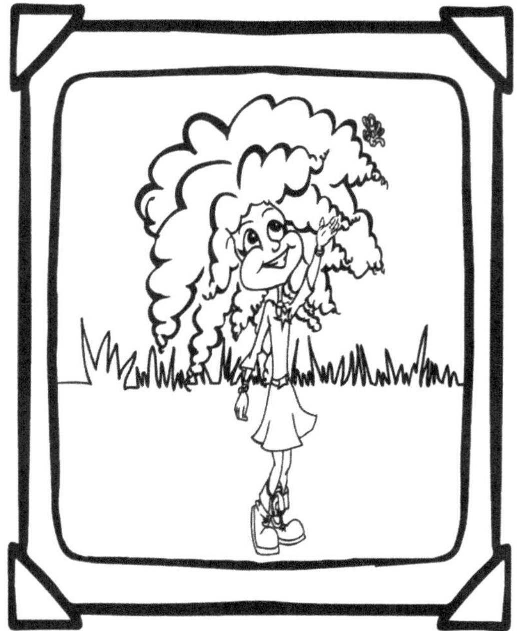

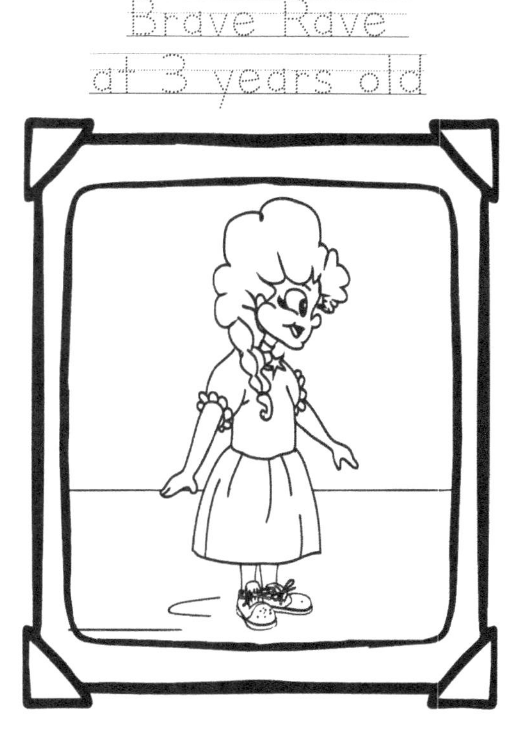

Brave Rave
at 8 years old

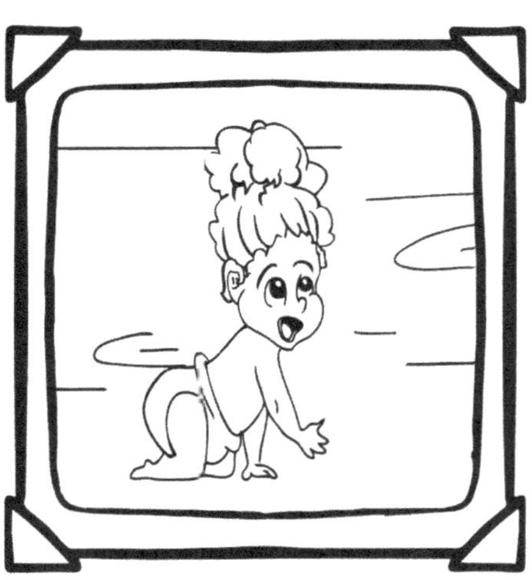

Brave Rave
at 6 months old

2

I can remember, smiling
at the moon and reaching
for the stars as a baby.

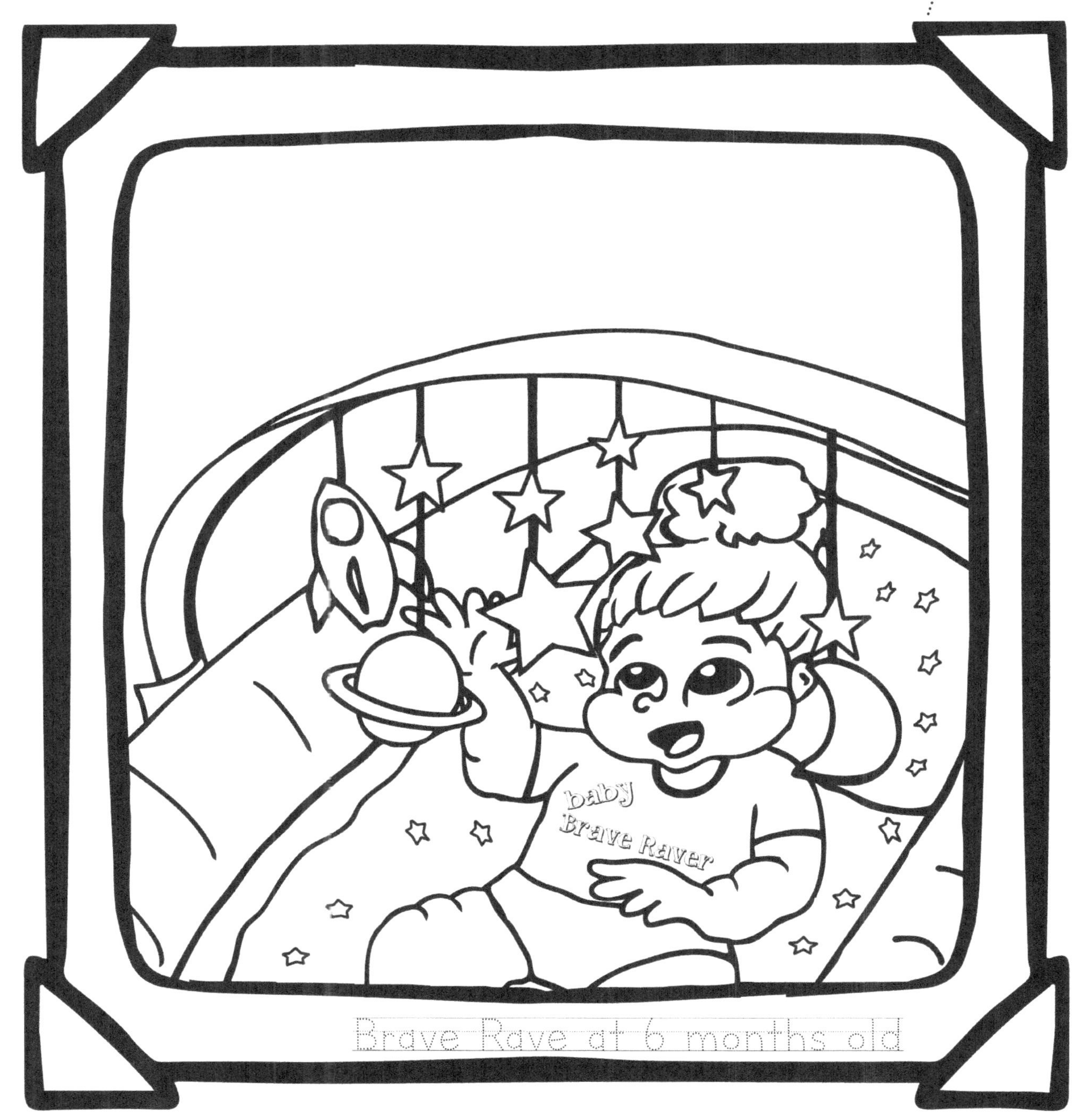

3

IMAGINE

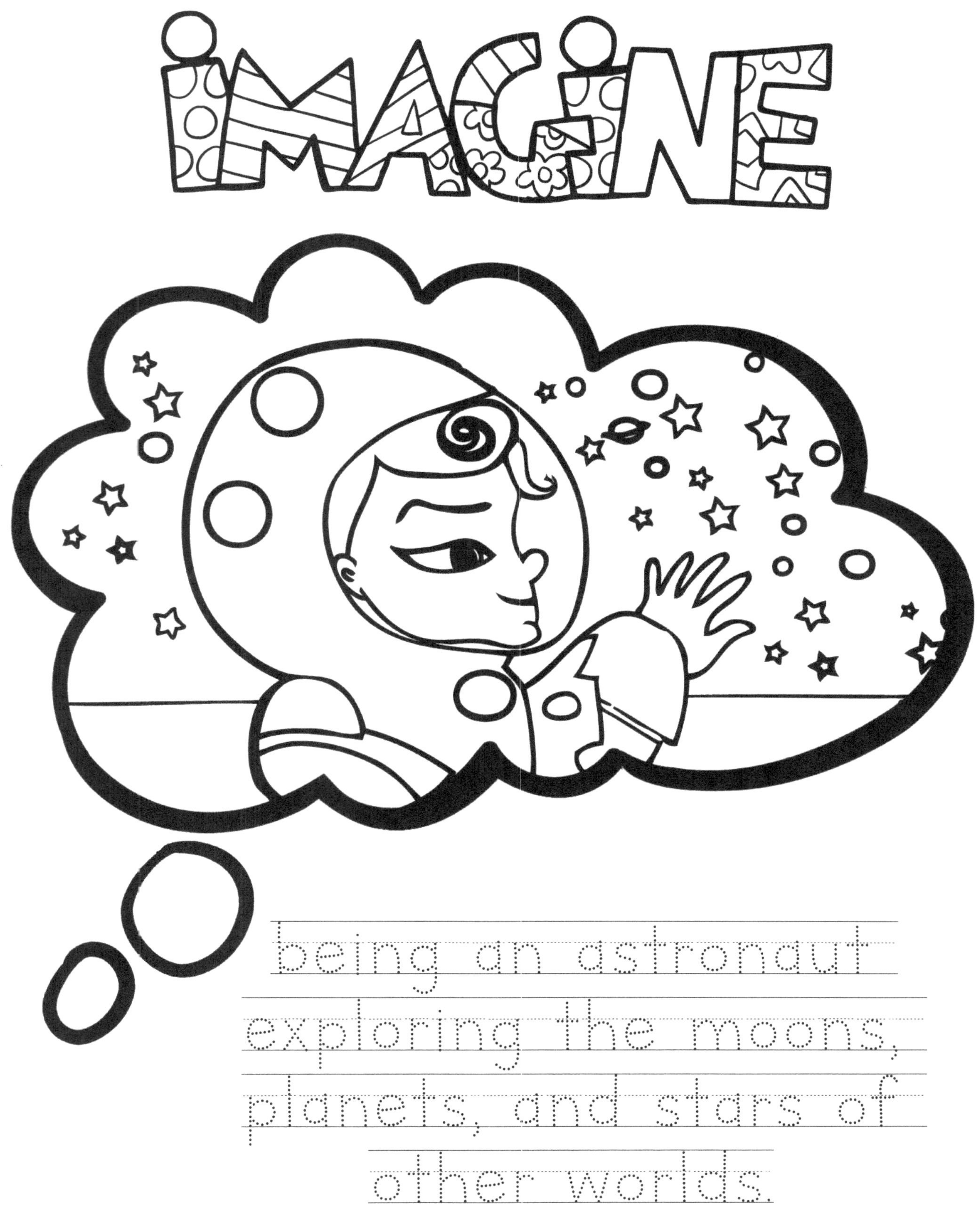

being an astronaut
exploring the moons,
planets, and stars of
other worlds.

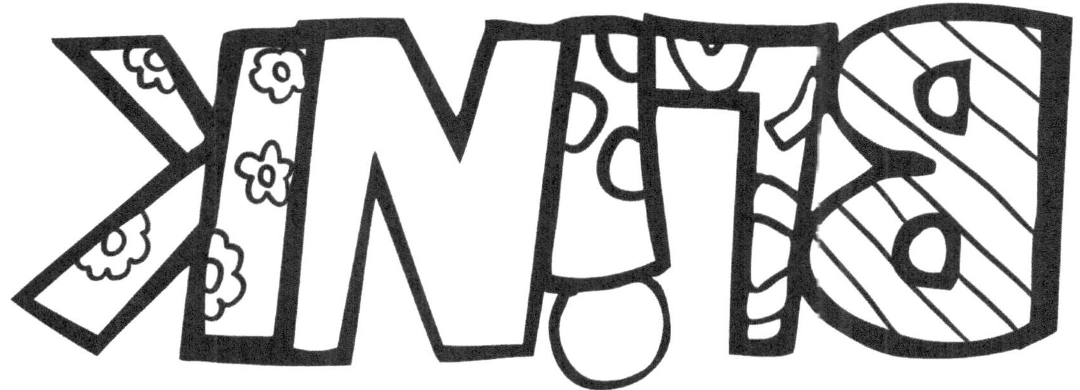

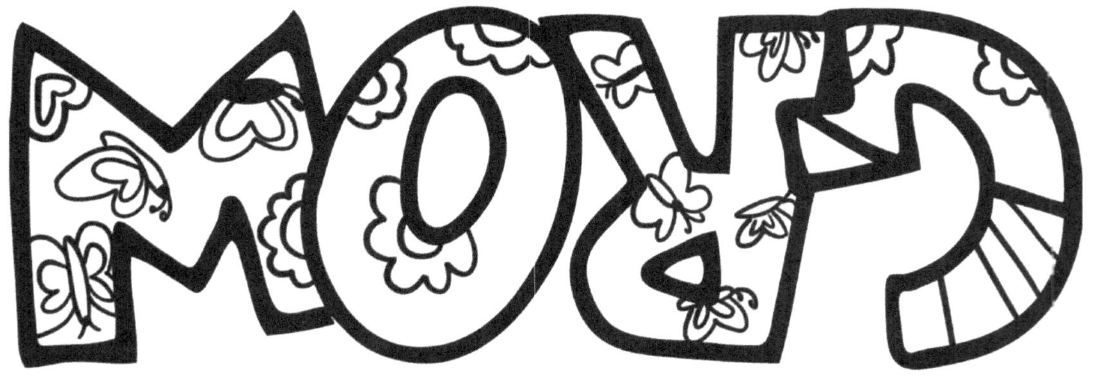

I join Mom in a nice yoga
stretch because it is good
for relaxing your mind and
your body. Mom says it helps
me to be my very BEST.

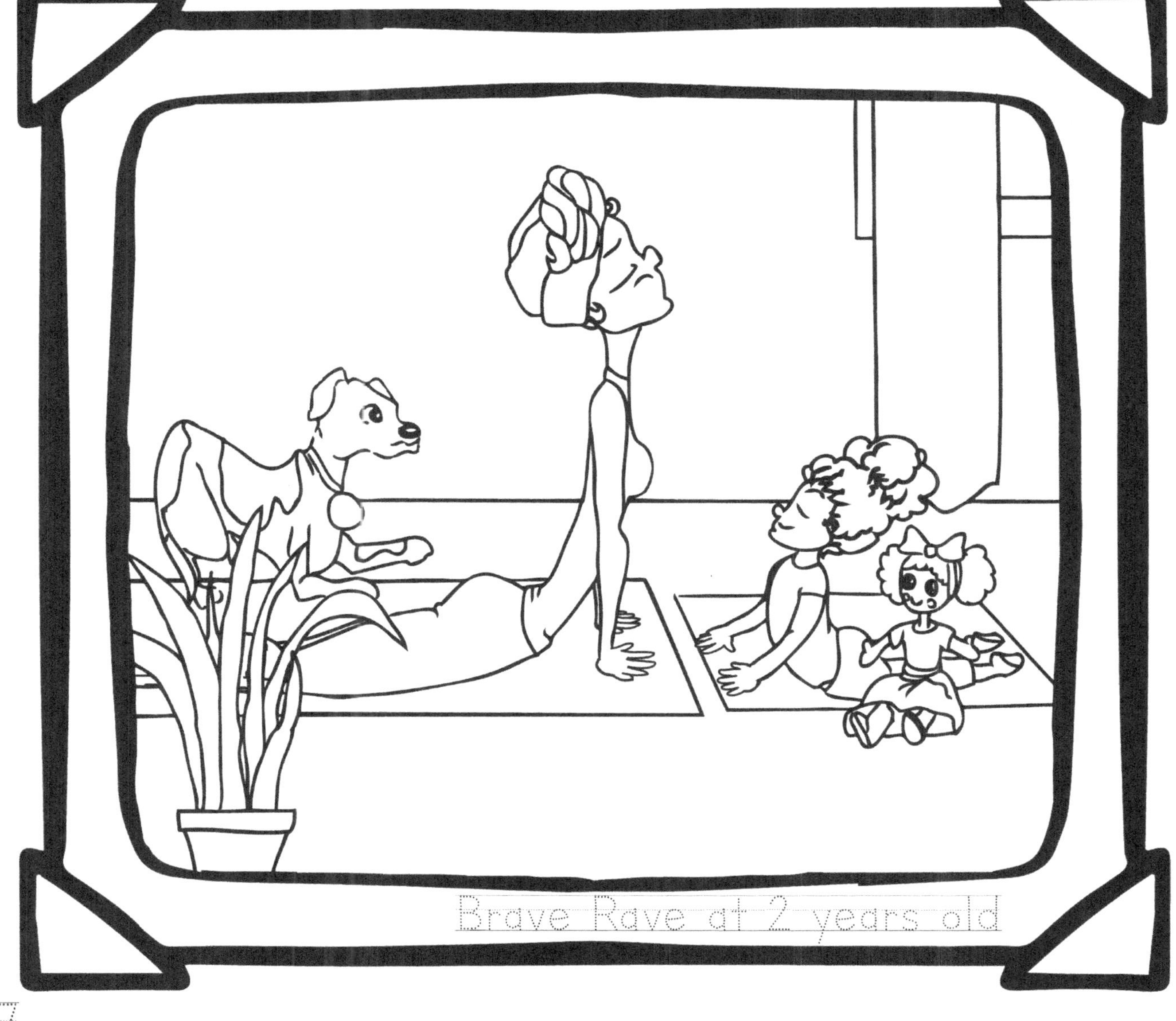

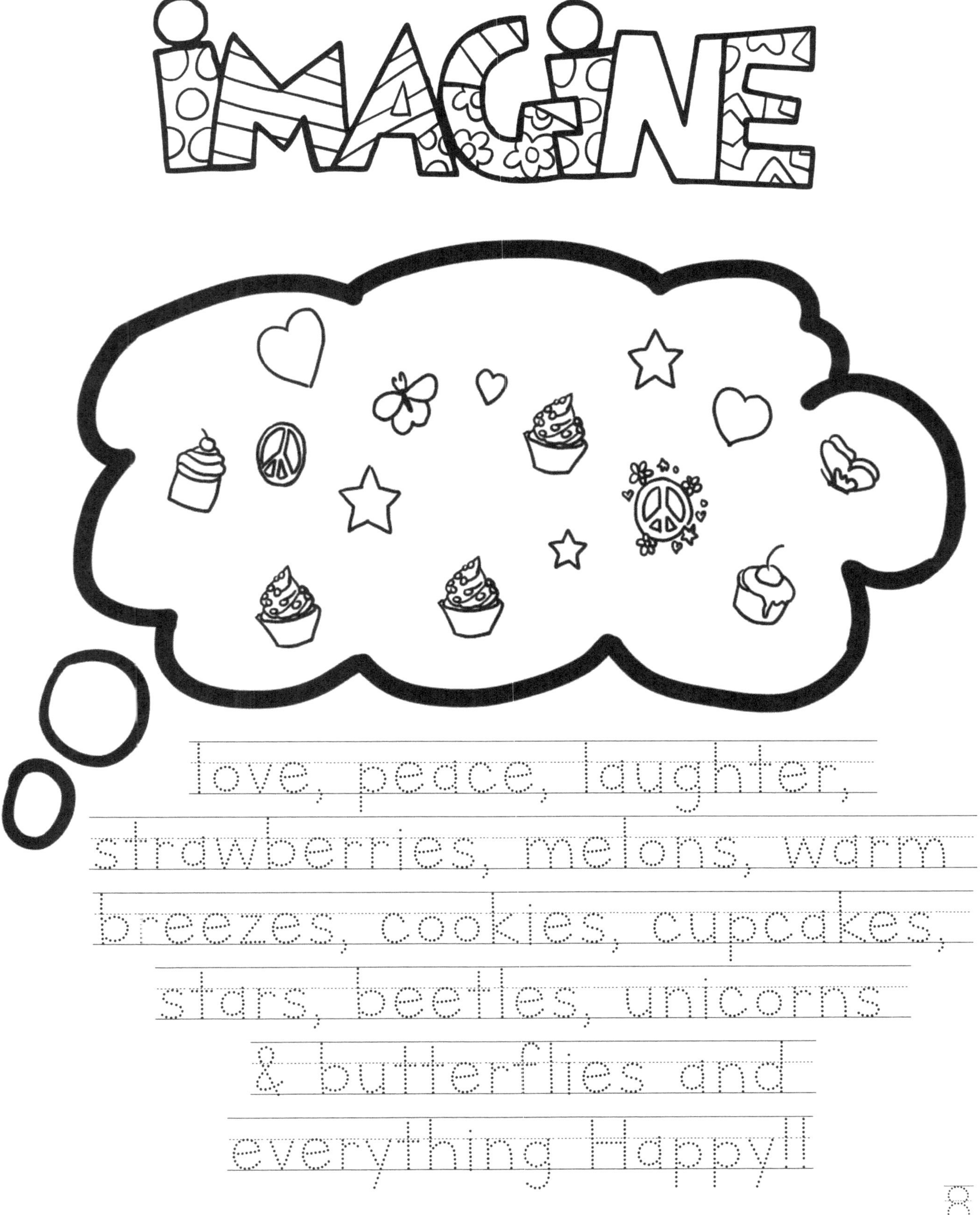

IMAGINE
love, peace, laughter,
strawberries, melons, warm
breezes, cookies, cupcakes,
stars, beetles, unicorns
& butterflies and
everything Happy!!

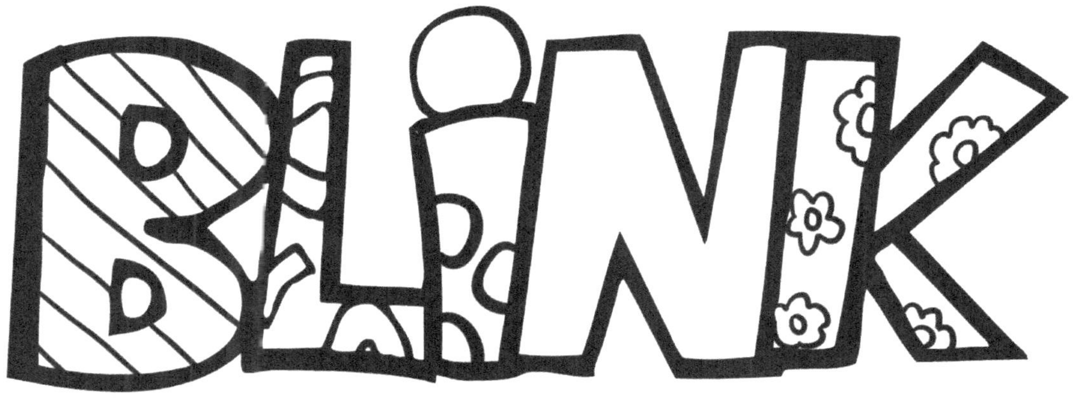
BLINK

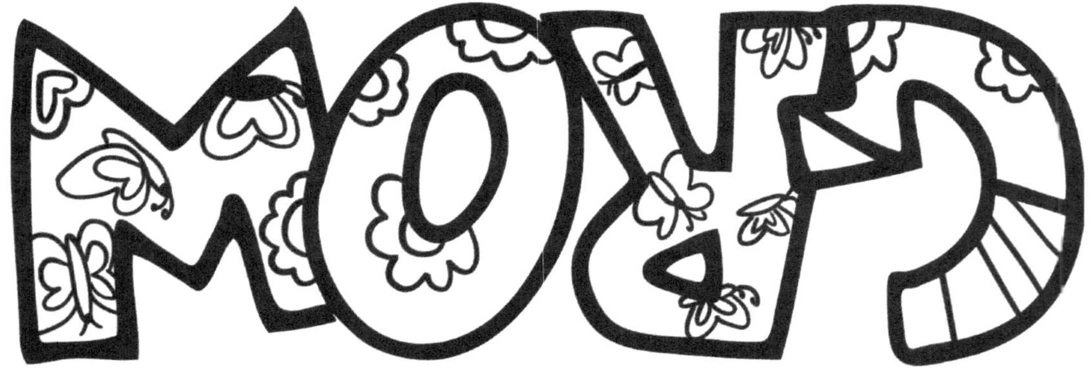

I tumble, twist,
turn, bend and flip
all over my room.

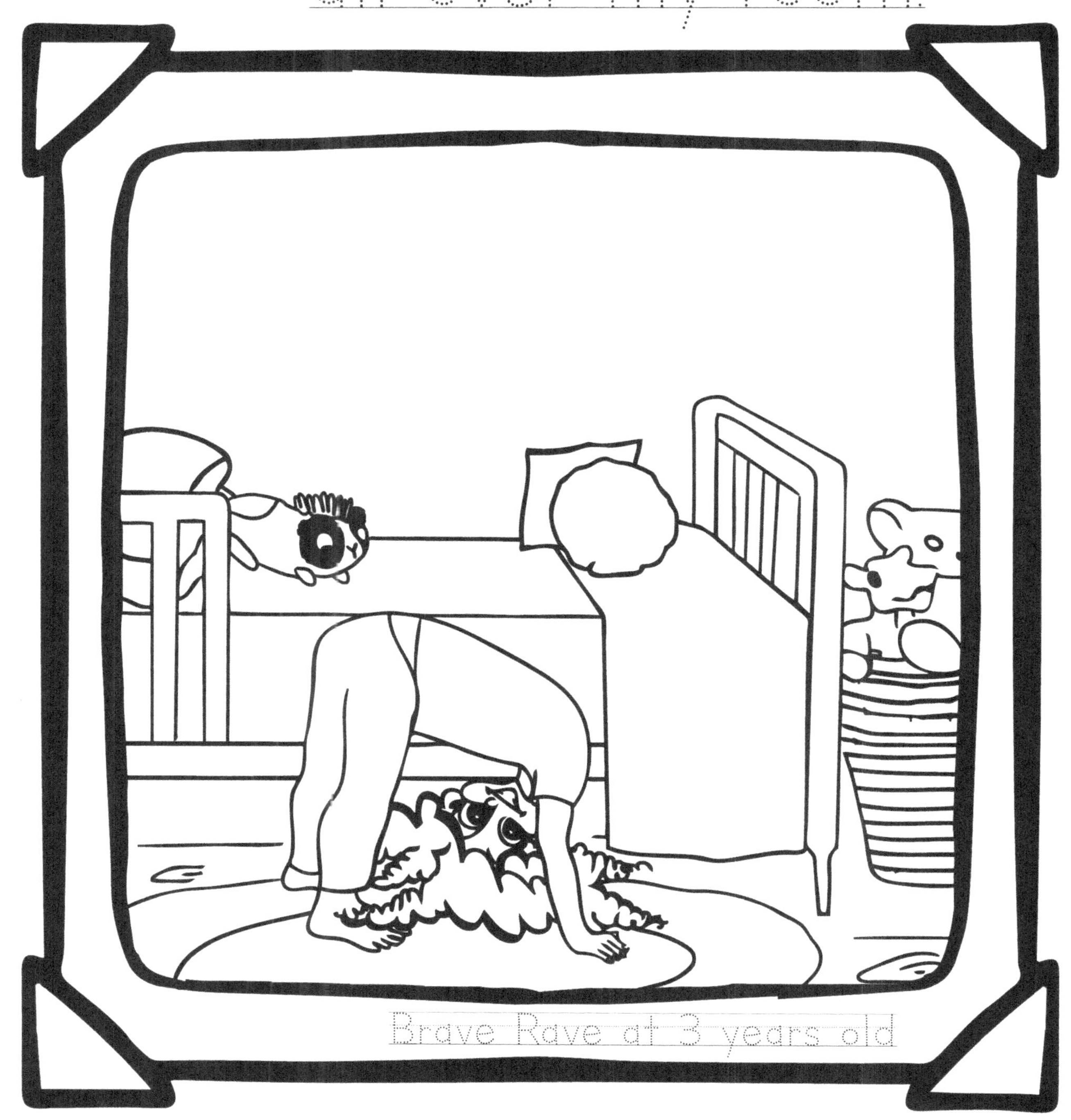

IMAGINE

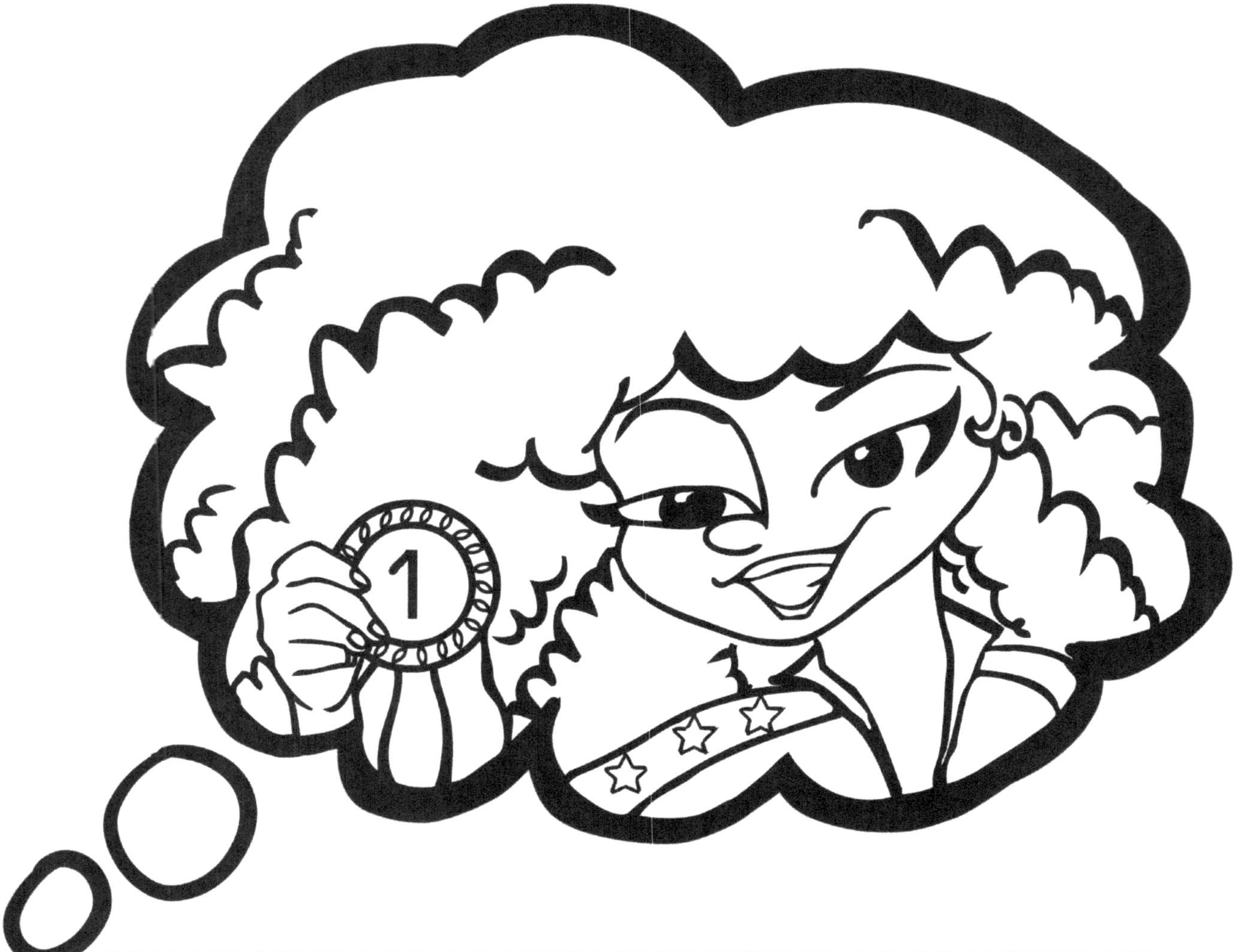

tumbling for a living and
being the very best Olympic
gymnast in the entire world!

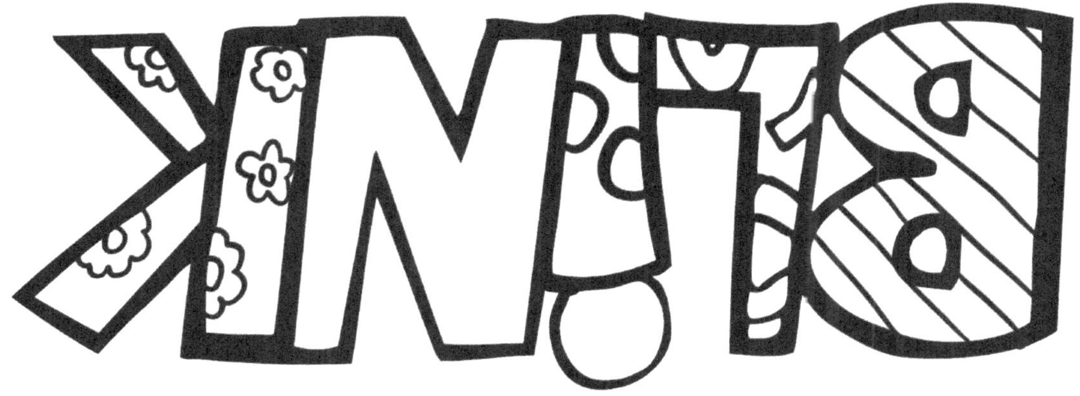
BLINK

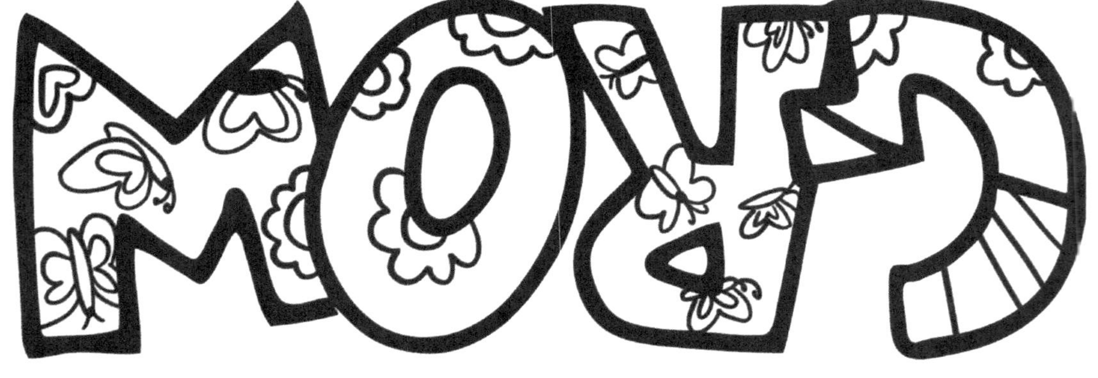
MOMS

I go to the bathroom to
brush, brush, brush, brush
my teeth so they can be
clean and sparkly.

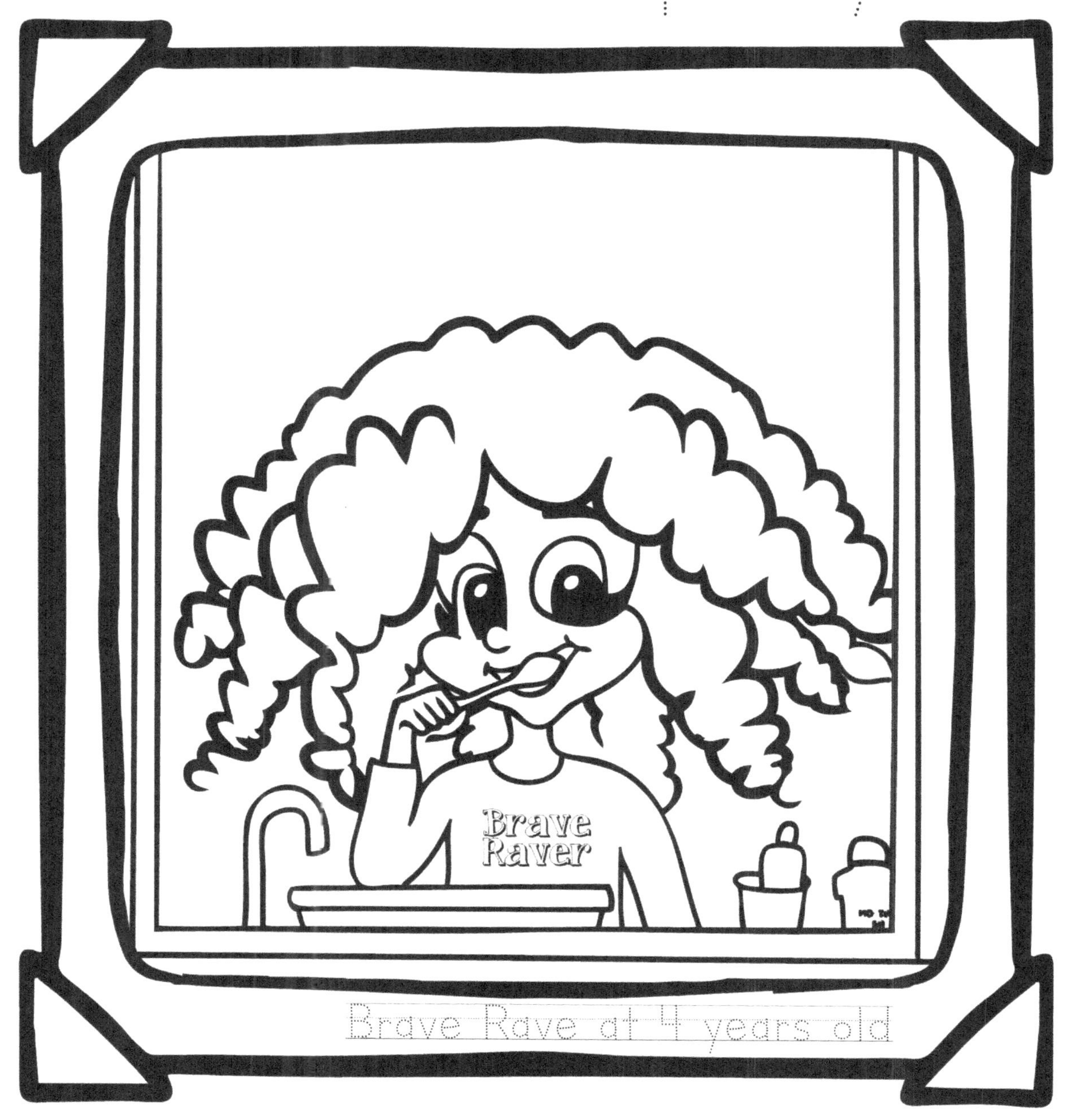

IMAGINE

being a super awesome dentist that helps people keep their teeth clean and healthy

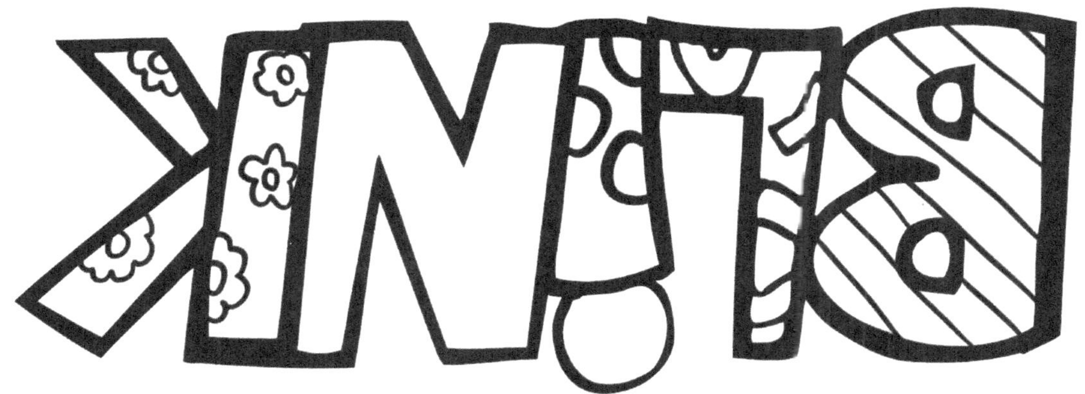
BLINK

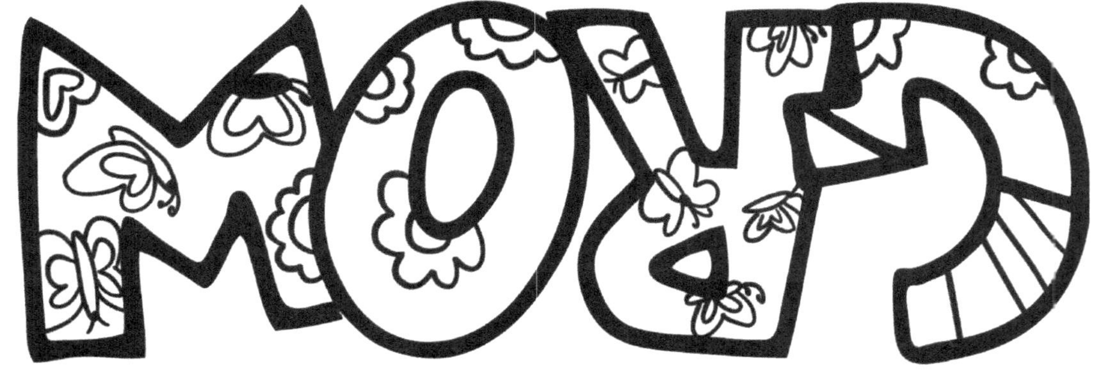
MOM

I have a great time as I splash-splash-splash in the bath. I must also keep clean and wash the day's dirt from my body.

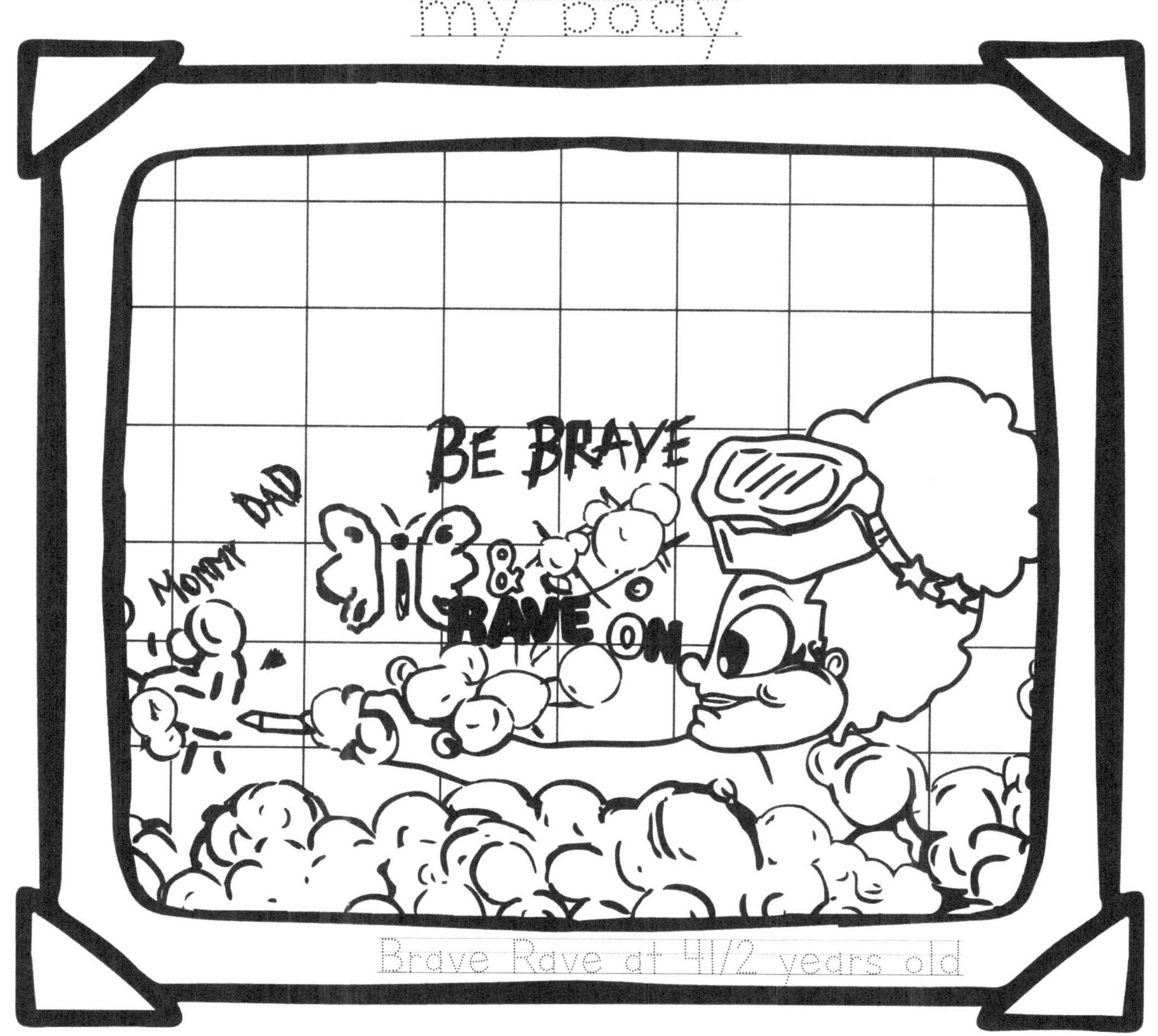

Brave Rave at 41/2 years old

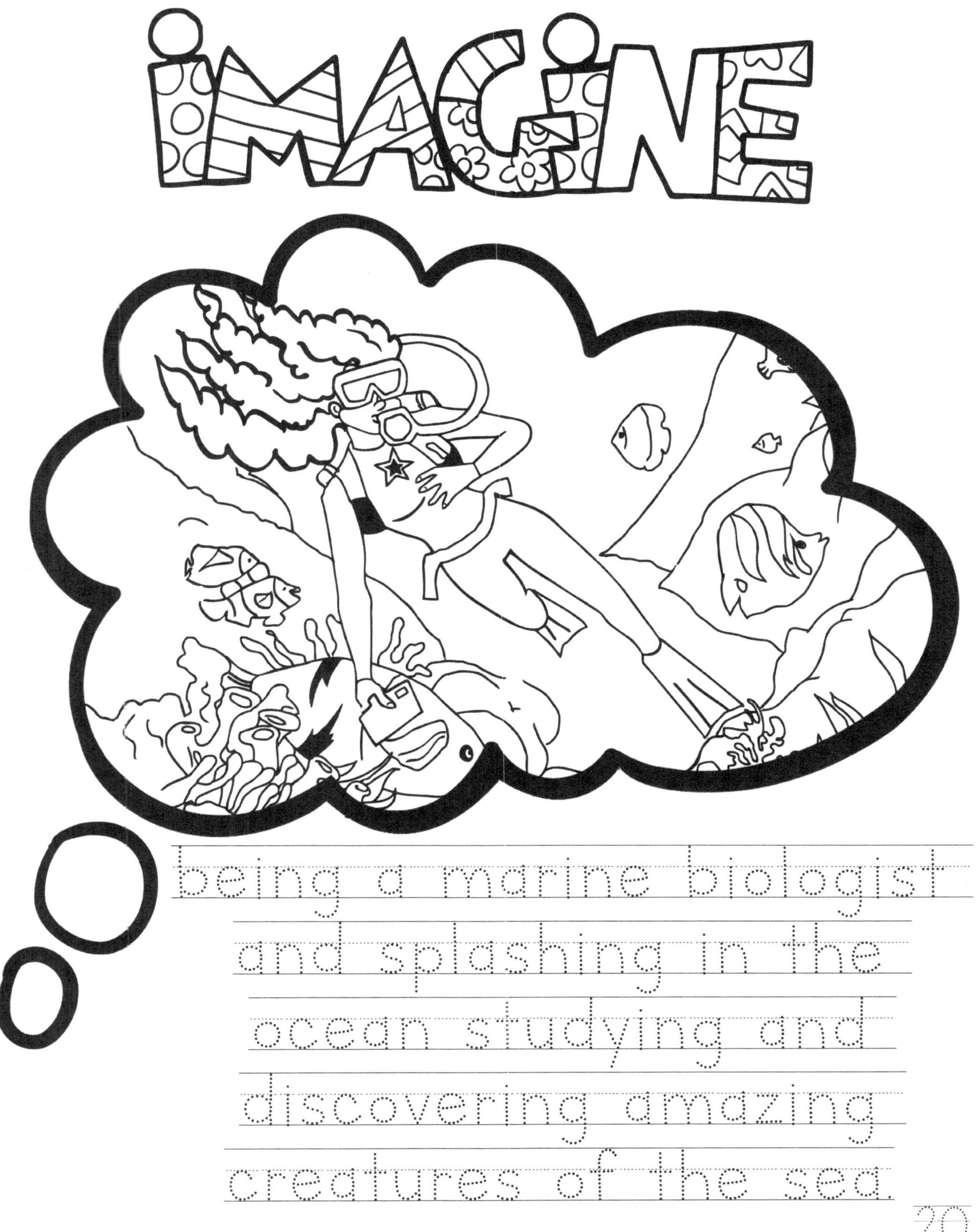

being a marine biologist
and splashing in the
ocean studying and
discovering amazing
creatures of the sea.

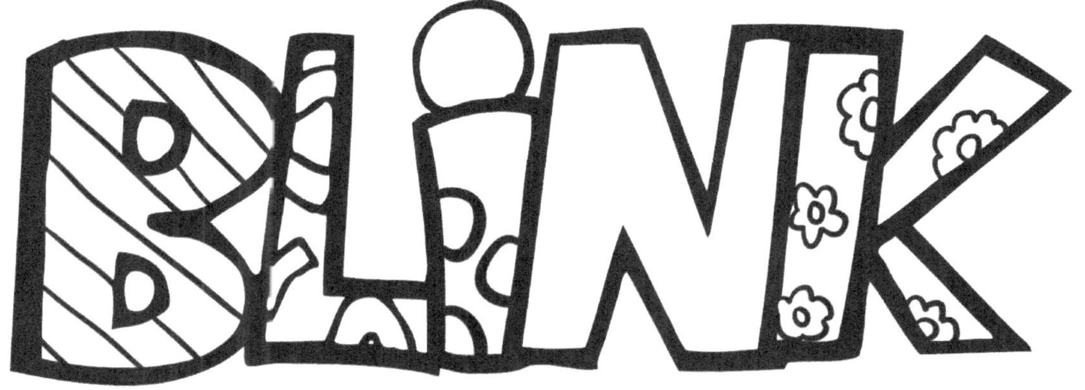

BLINK

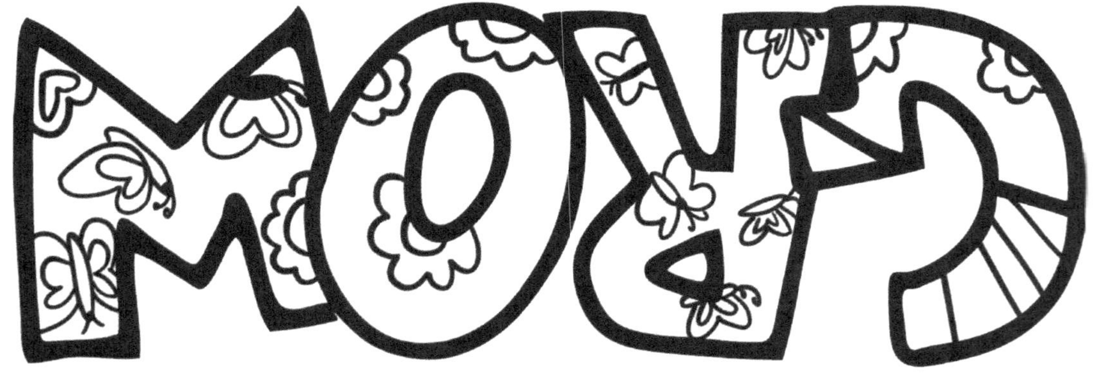

MOM

I grab my paper, pencil, and crayons to draw-draw-draw-draw because it is fun. Drawing makes me happy.

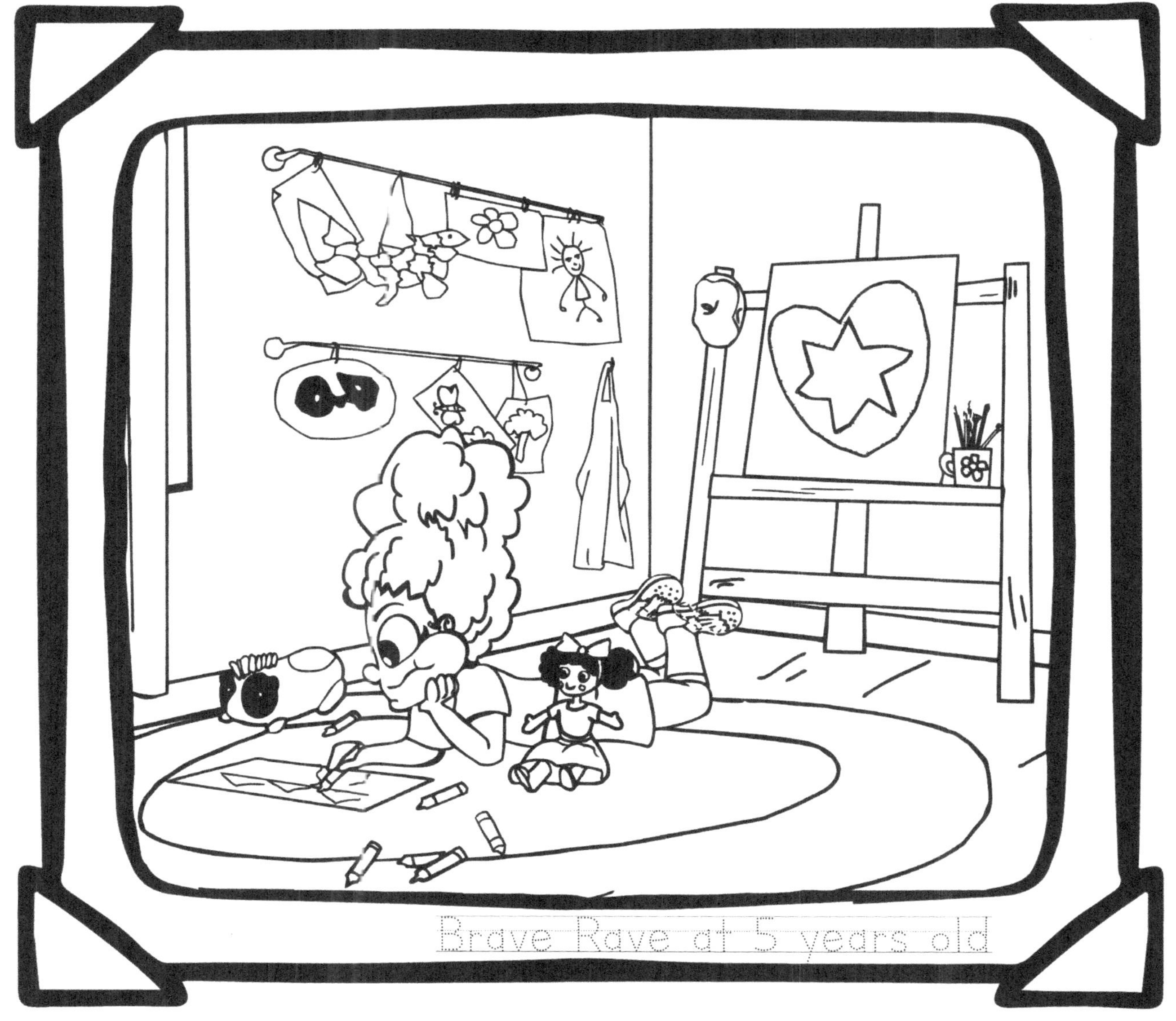

23

iMAGiNE

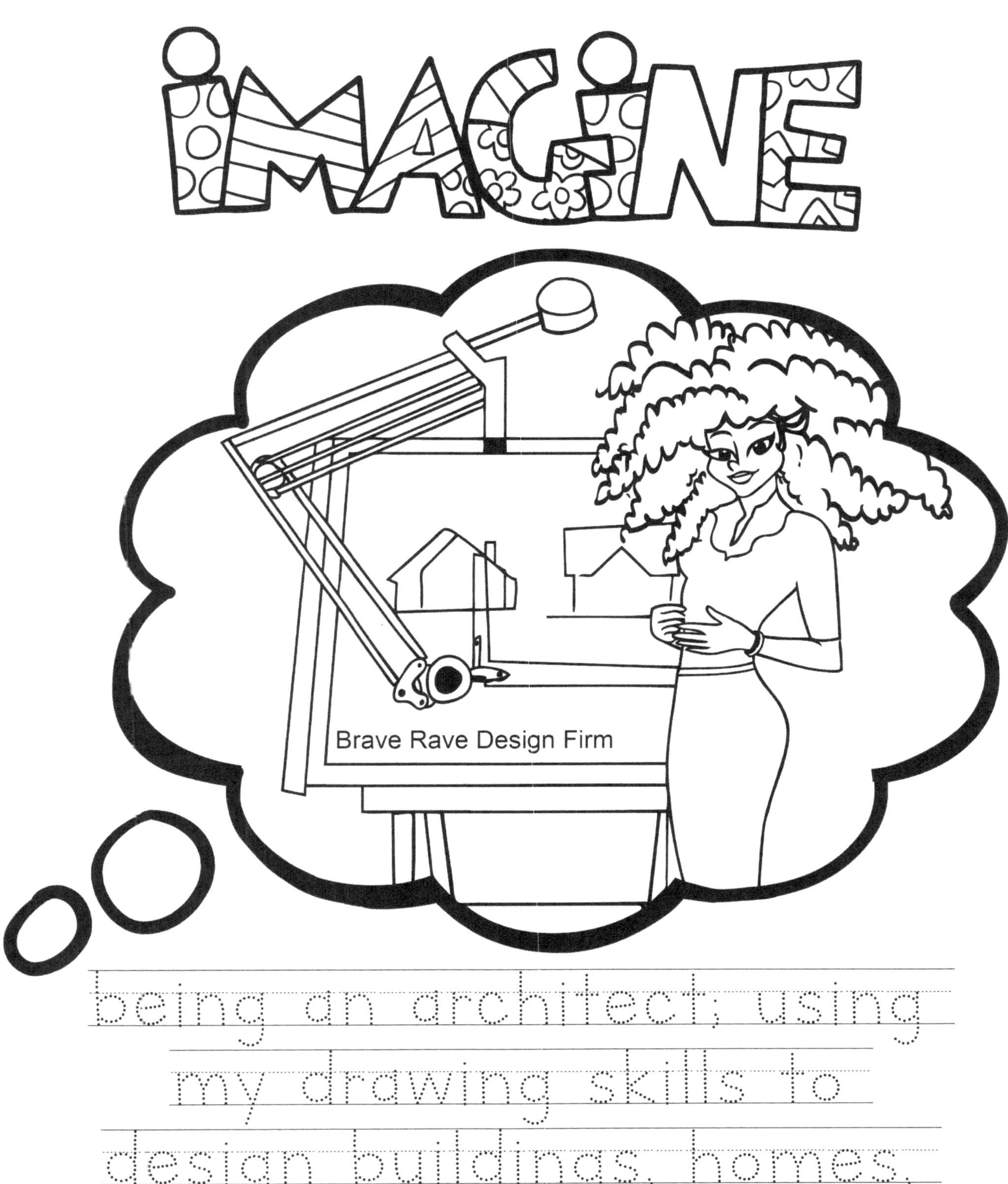

being an architect; using
my drawing skills to
design buildings, homes,
neighborhoods, and cities

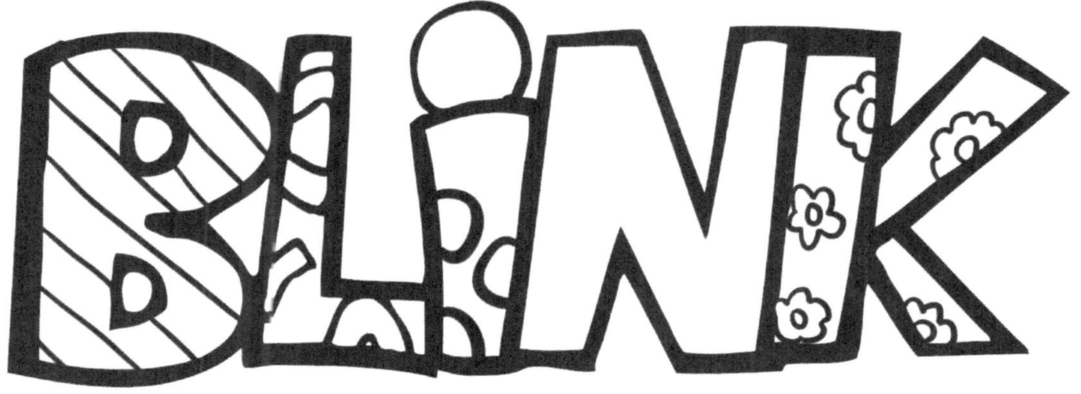
BLINK

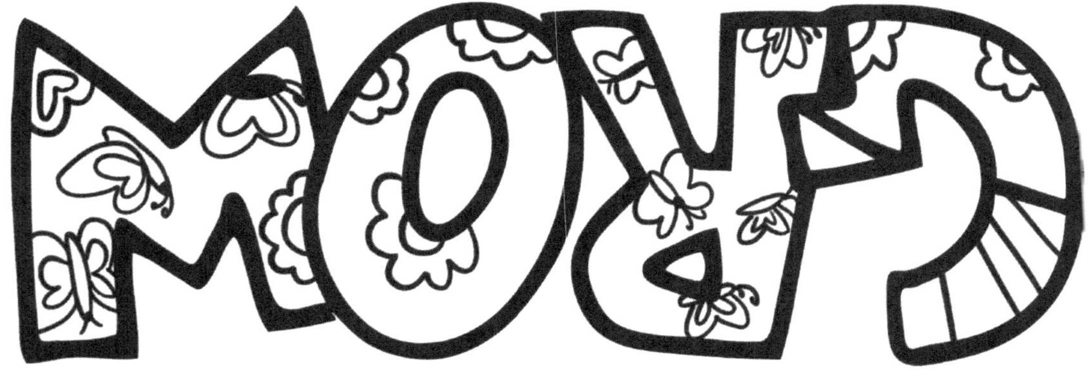

I put on my prettiest, most
Feel-Good outfit for the day.

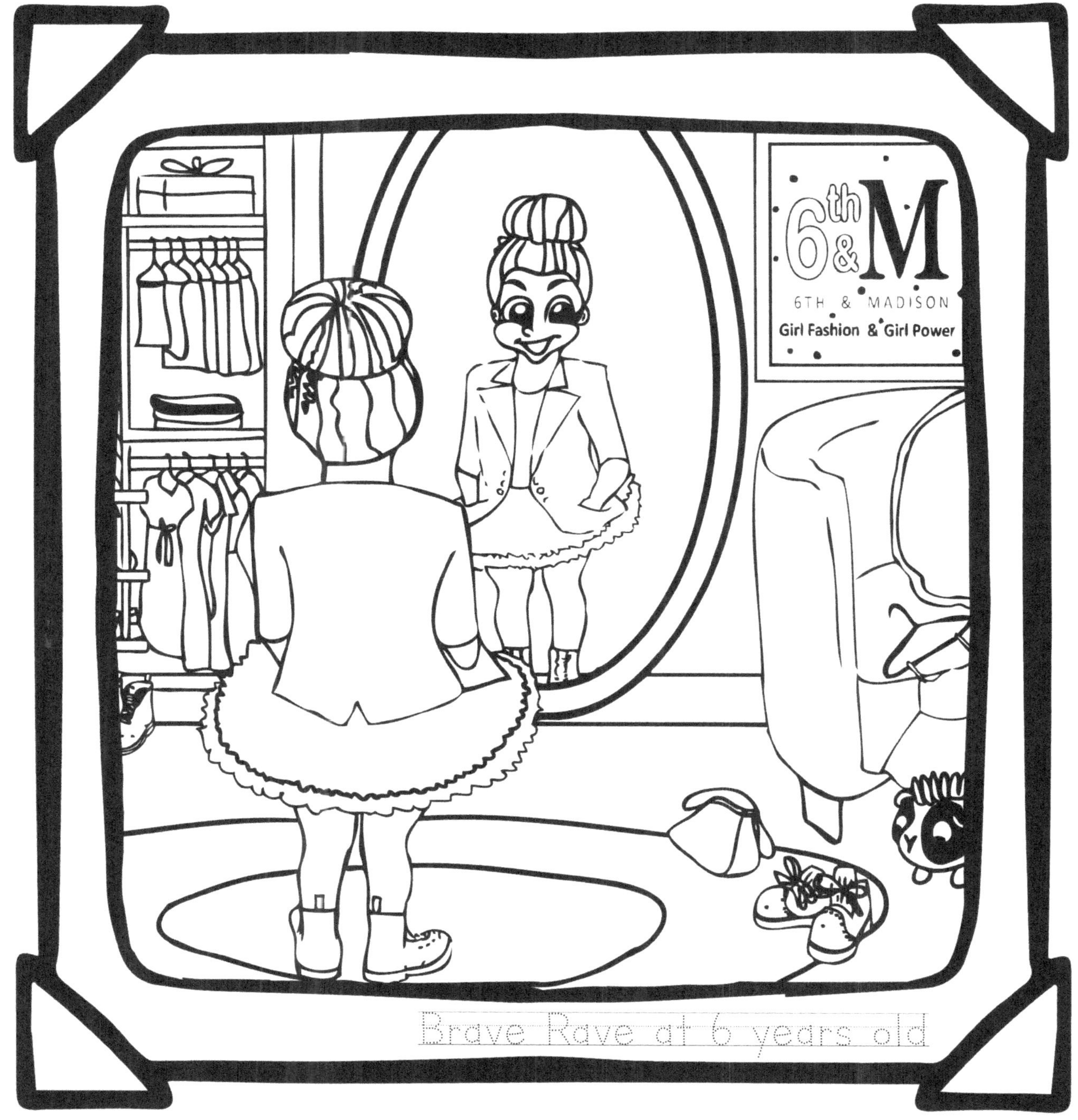

being a super model
walking down runways or a
fashion designer showing off
my beautifully crafted designs
to people from all over
the world

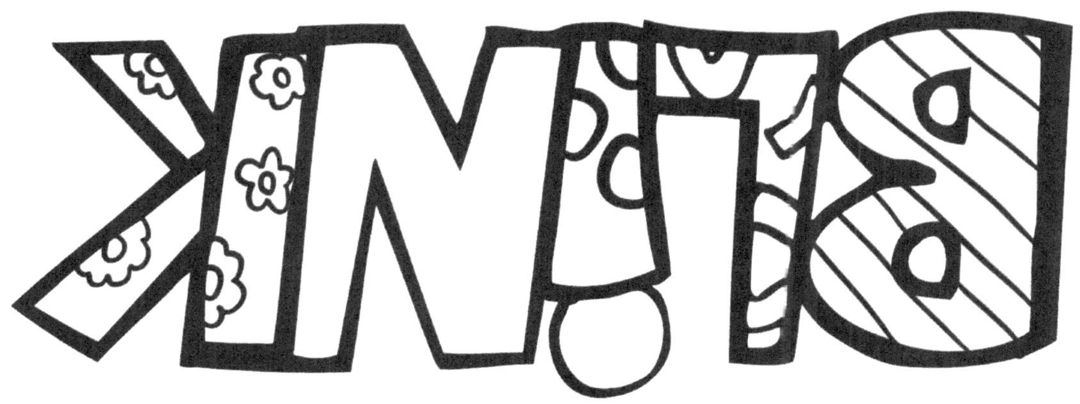

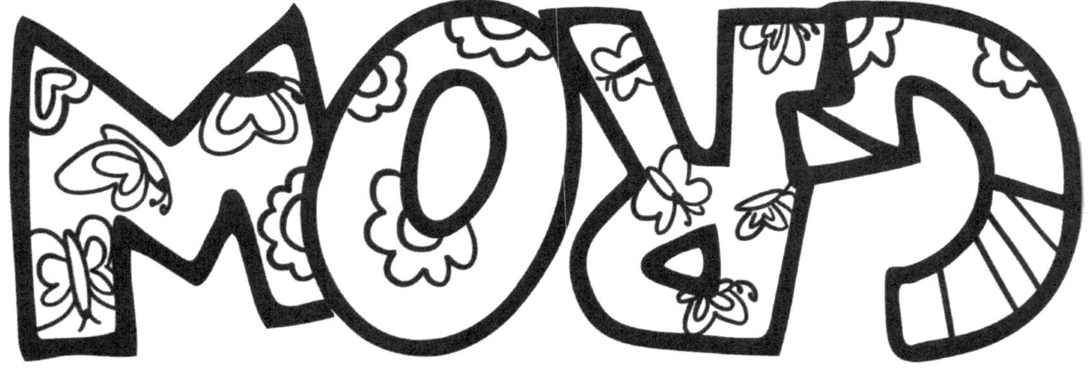

Dad is in the garden. I help
him to dig-dig-dig in the dirt
to plant fruits and vegetables
that we will one day use to
prepare healthy meals.

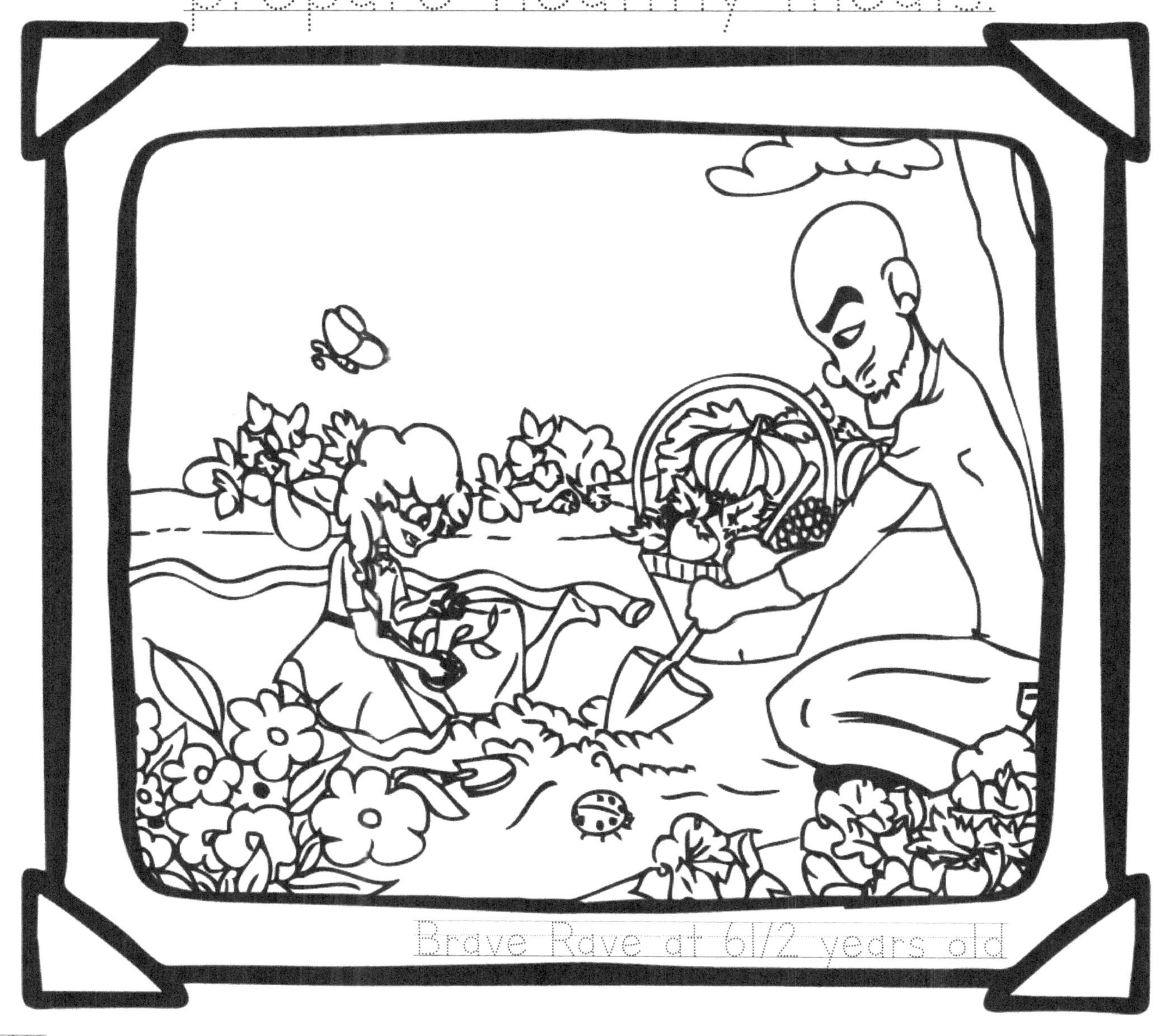

31

IMAGINE

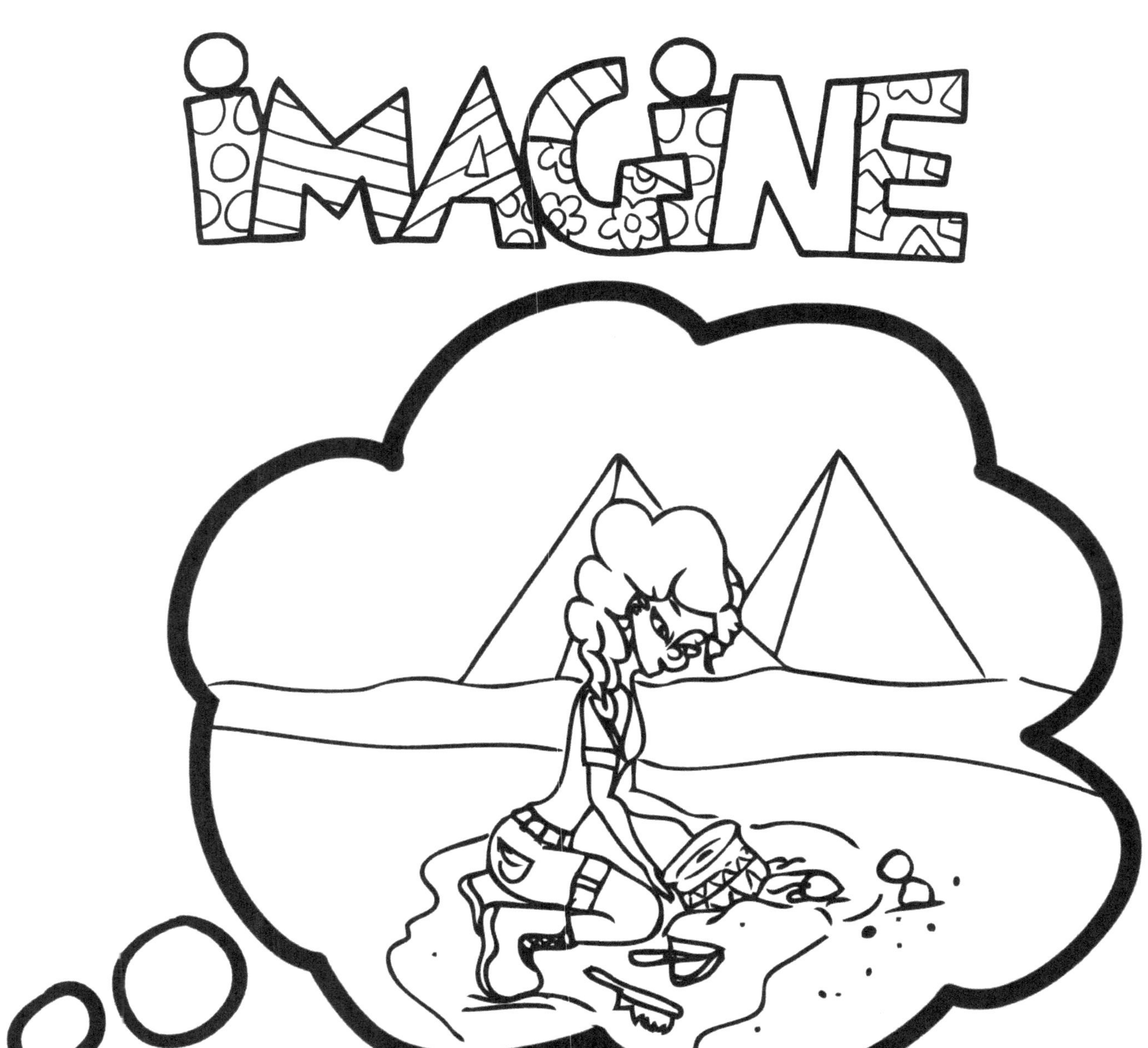

being an archeologist in Africa, uncovering ancient artifacts buried in the dirt and sand

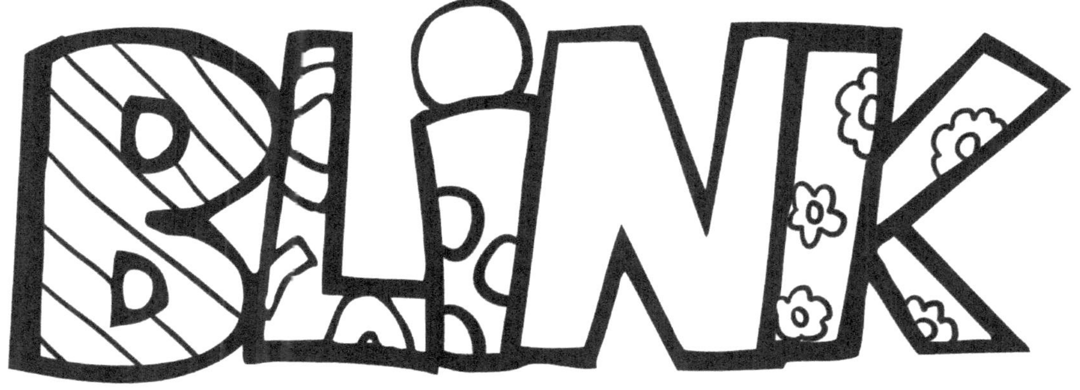
BLINK

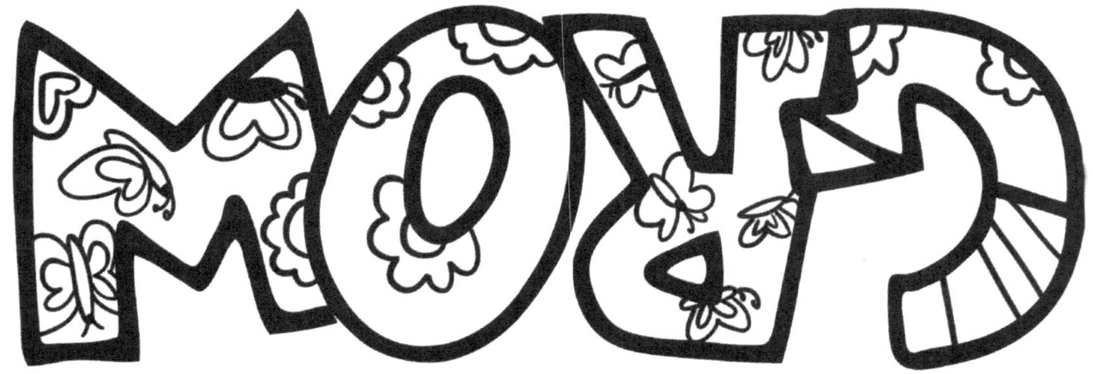

I help my parents prepare delicious meals made from fresh fruits and vegetables gathered from our garden to keep us energized and healthy.

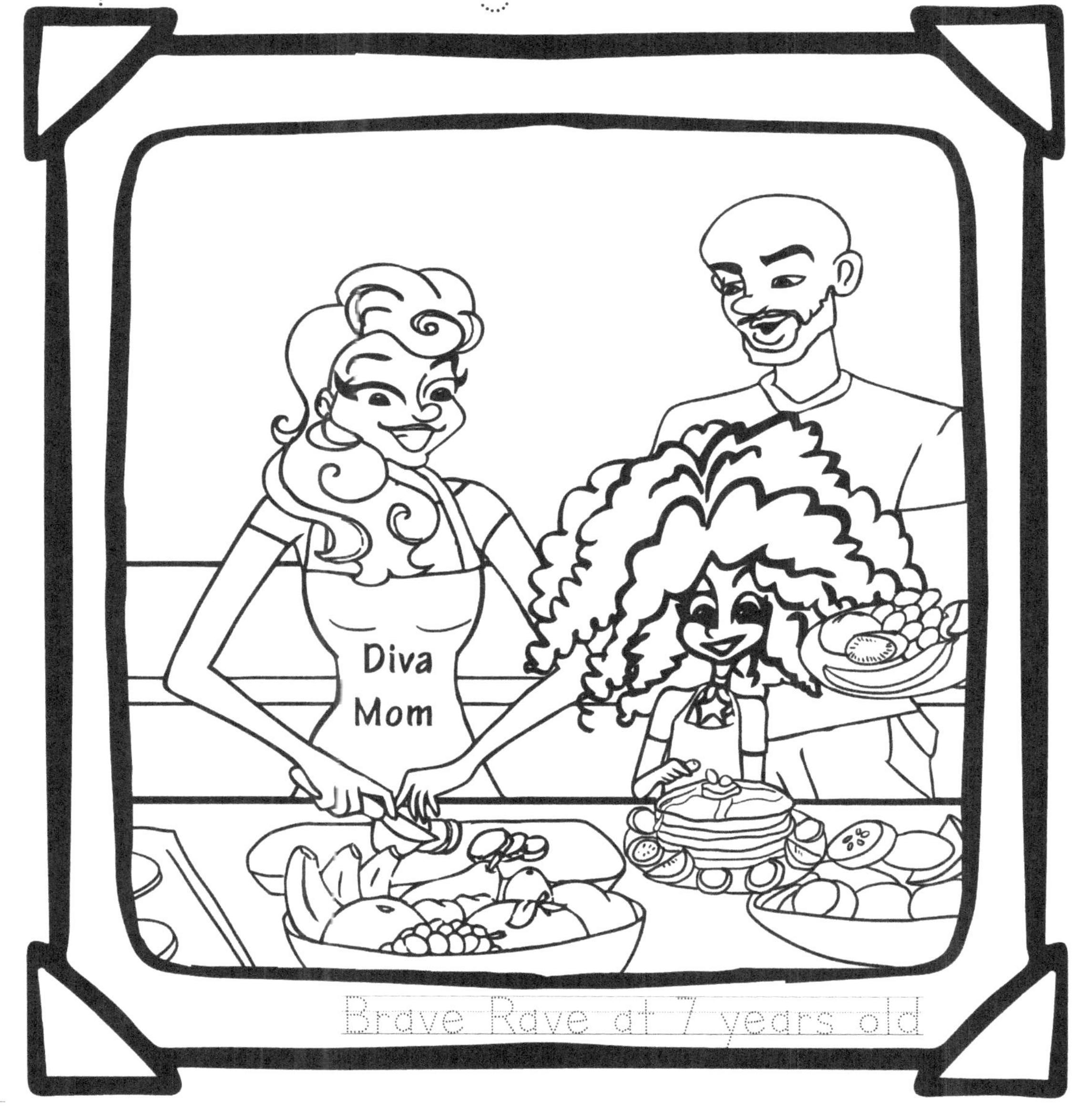

iMAGiNE

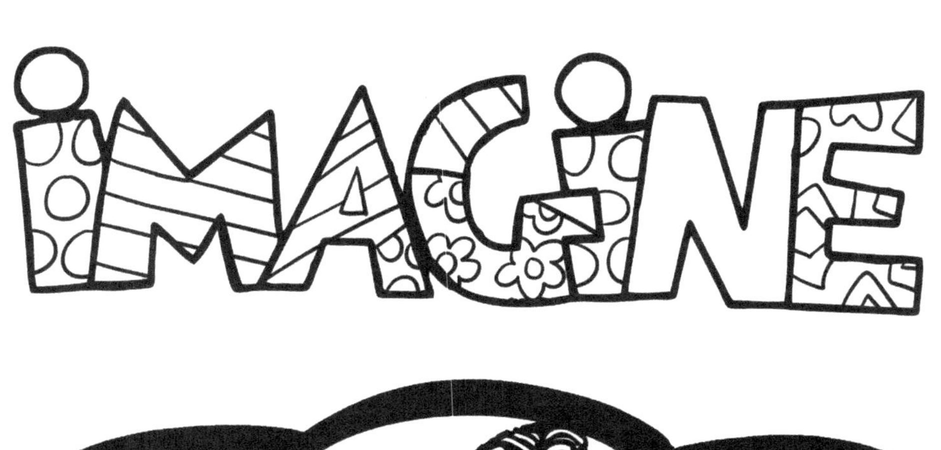

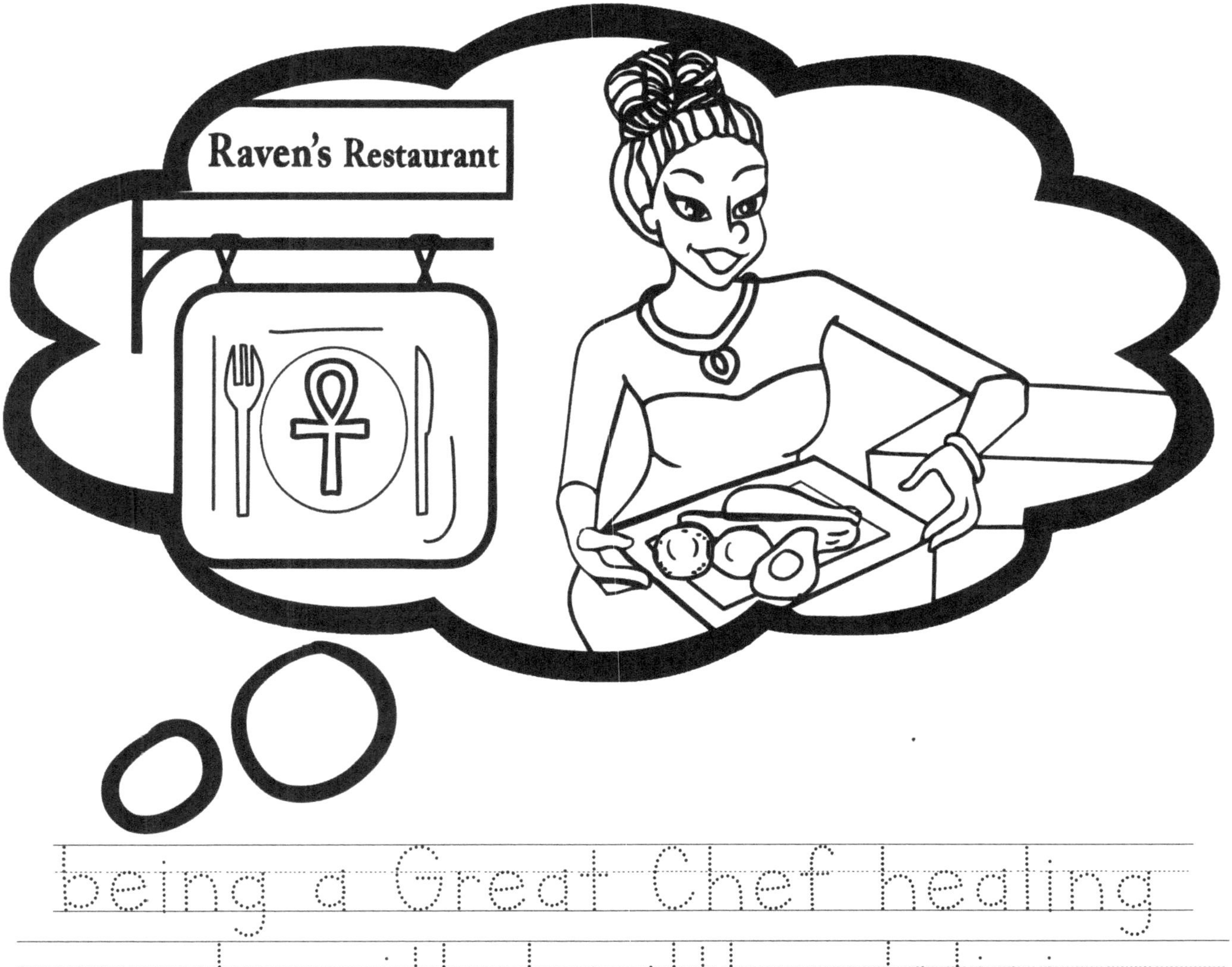

being a Great Chef healing
people with healthy delicious
magical fruits and vegetables
from the Earth.

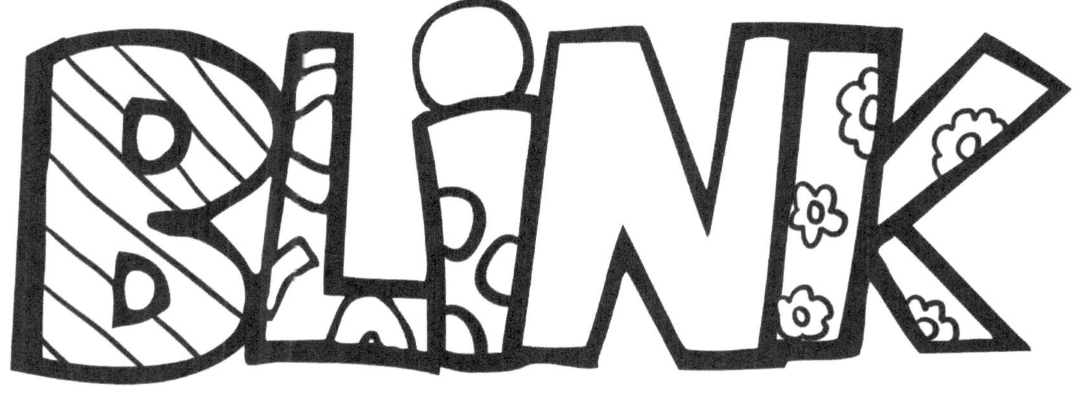
BLINK

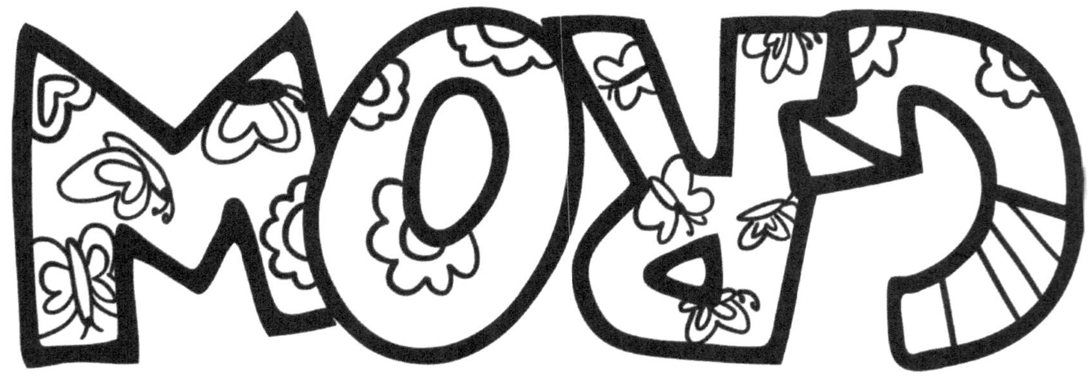

Mom does my hair to keep it healthy and growing. It makes me feel like Royalty. She says my hair is my true crown and to treat it with great care.

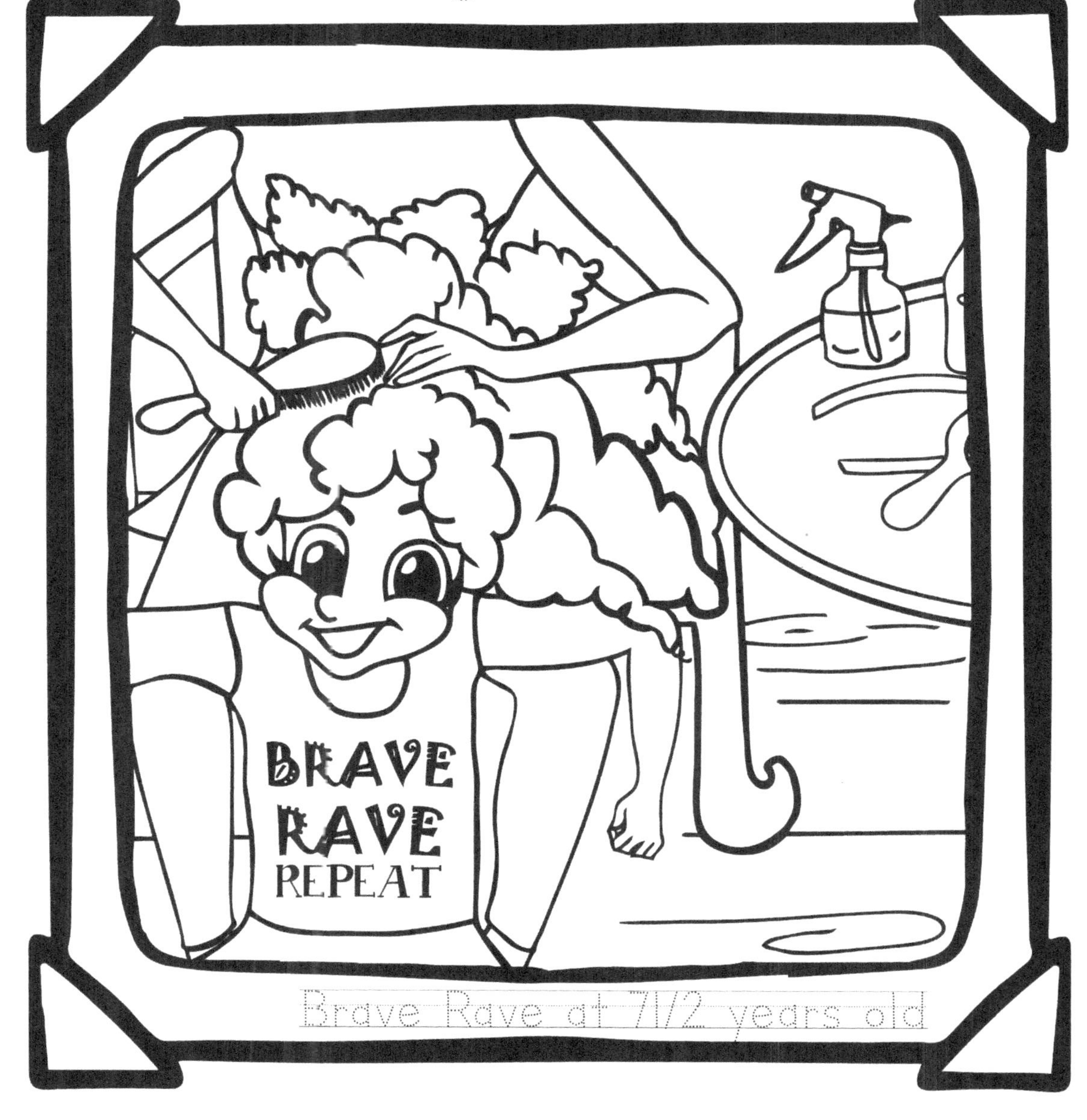

Brave Rave at 7 1/2 years old

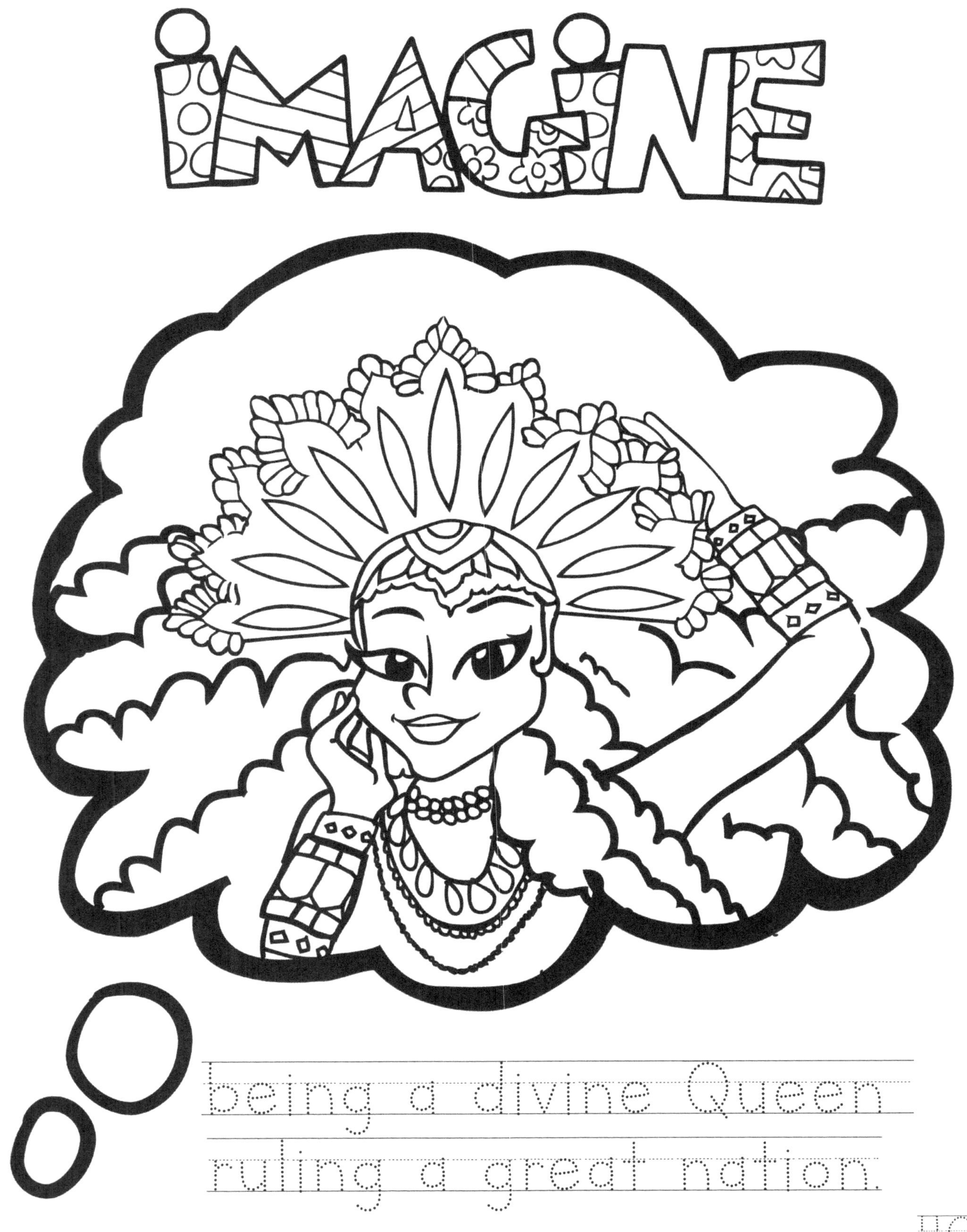

IMAGINE
being a divine Queen
ruling a great nation.

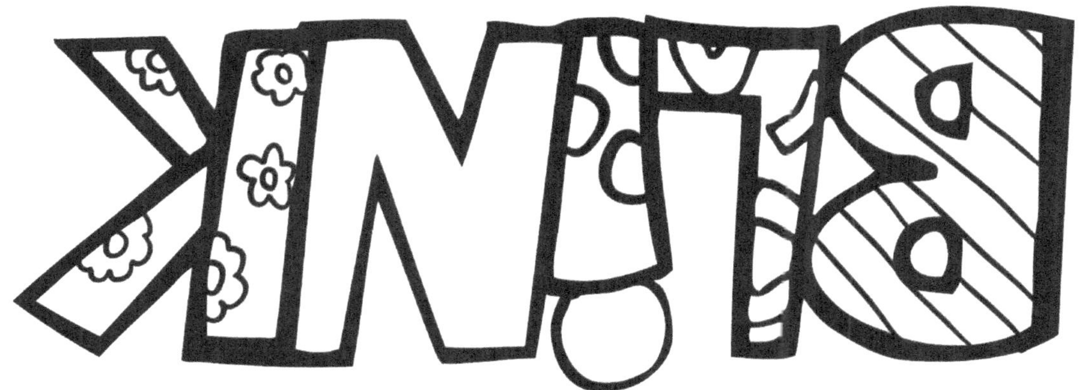

BLINK

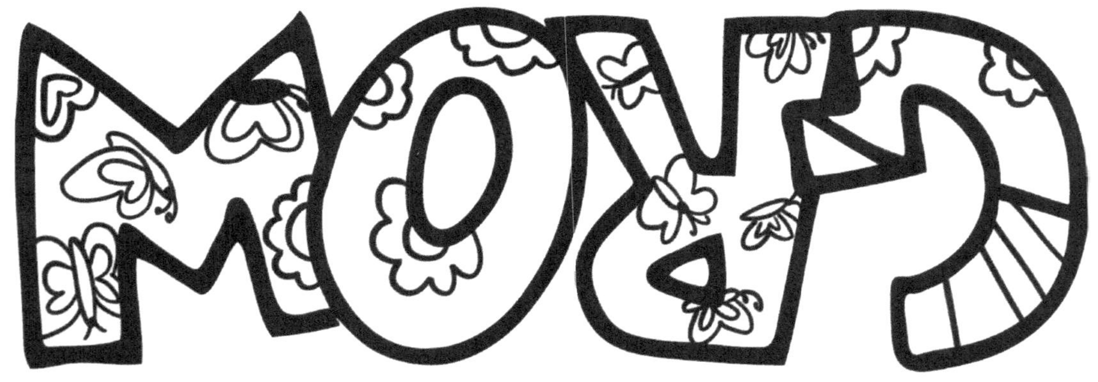

I always take time to practice
my Dance-Dance-Dance-Dance.
It keeps my body healthy

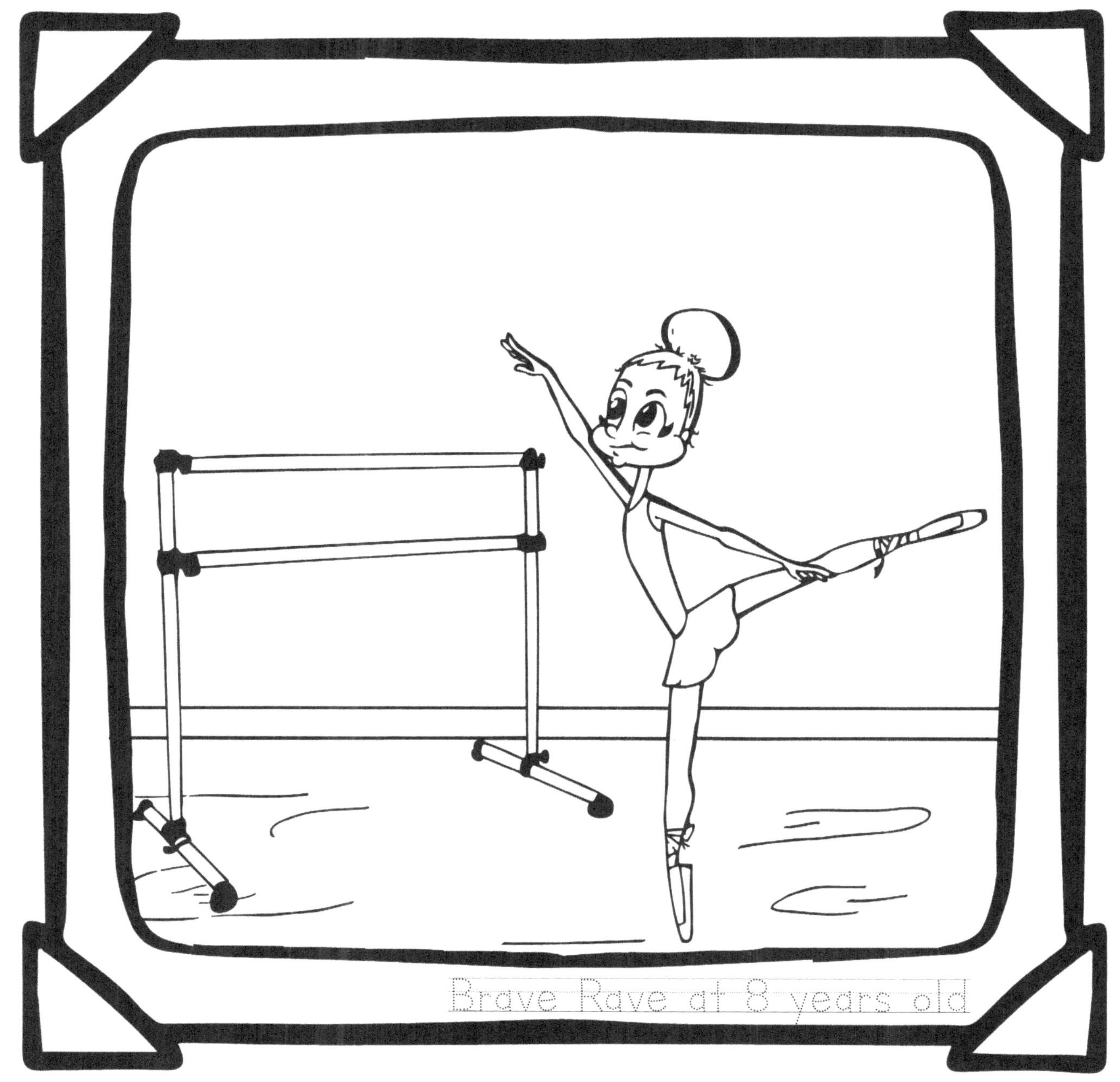

IMAGINE

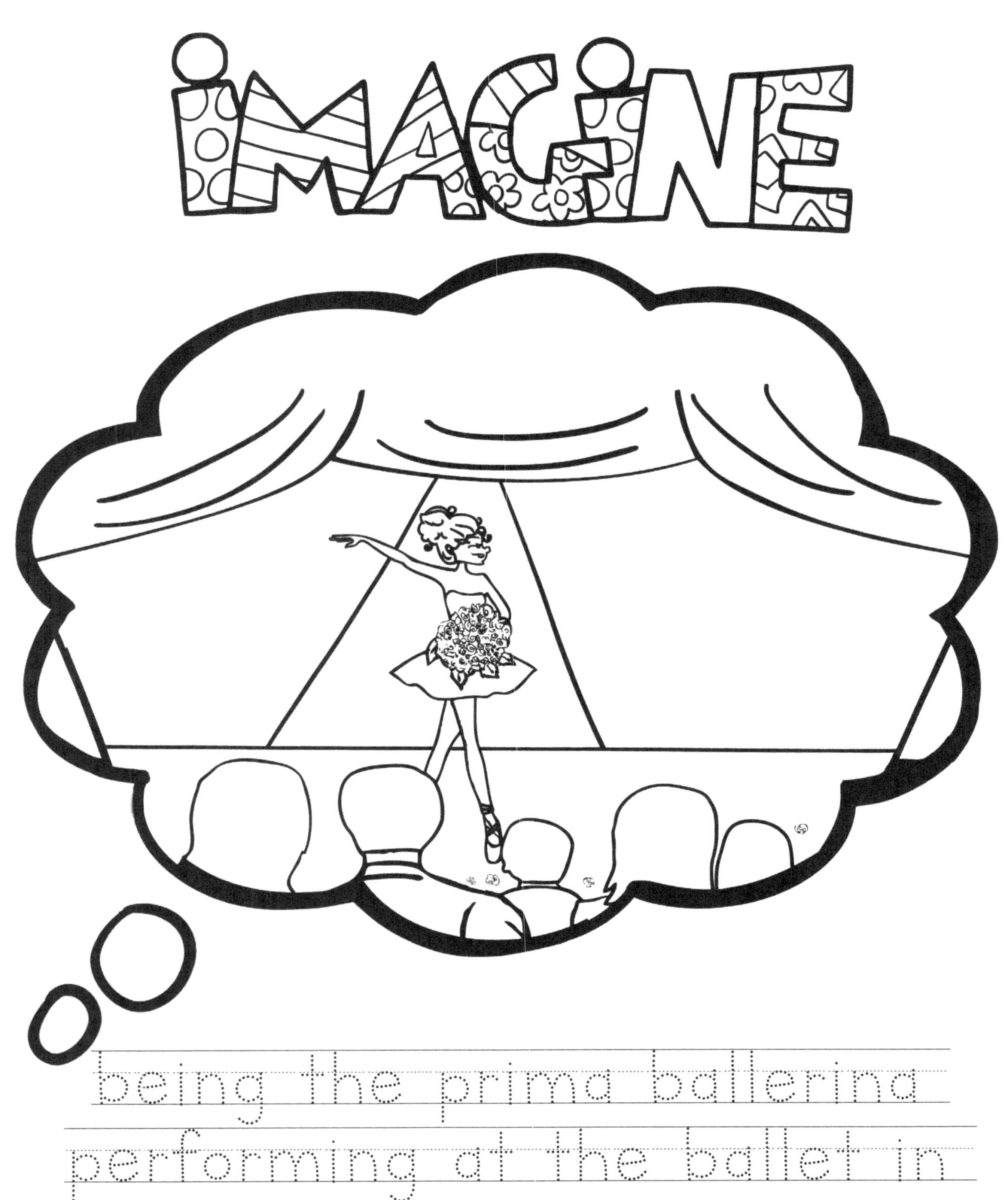

being the prima ballerina performing at the ballet in front of a huge audience.

44

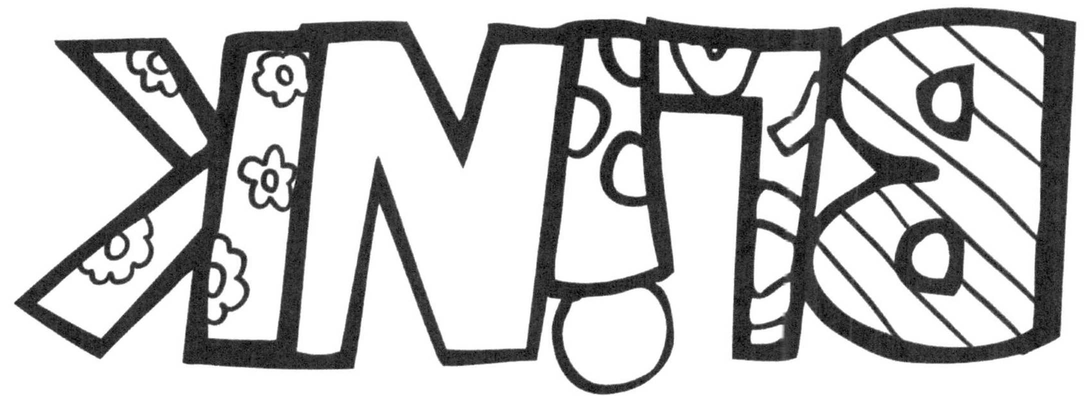
BLINK

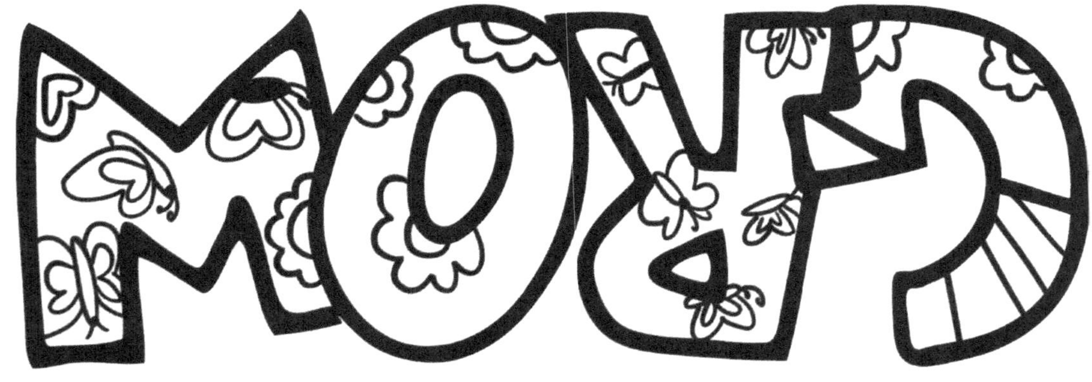

MOM

I write all of my day's
thoughts, feelings, and dreams
in my diary.

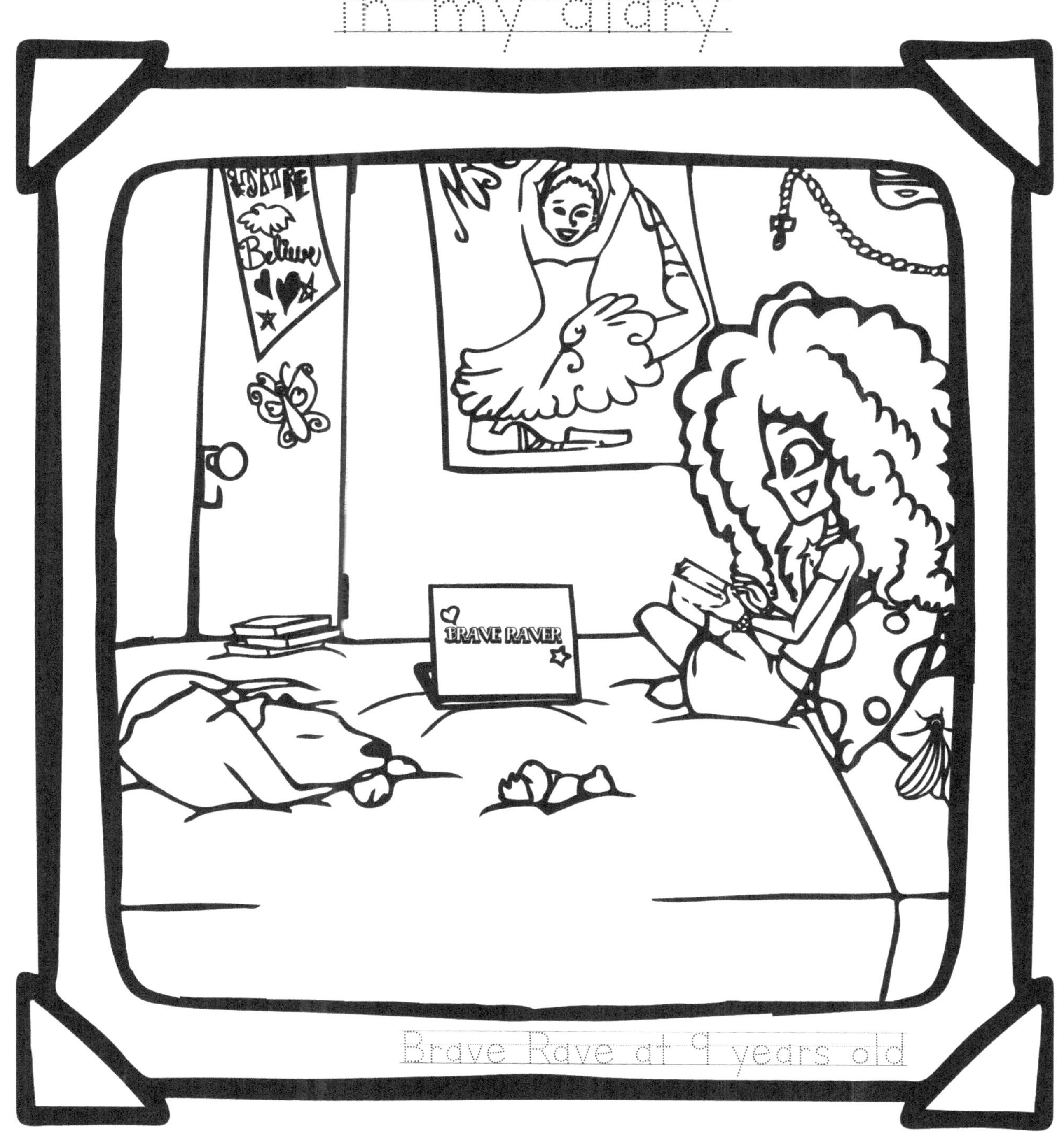

iMAGiNE

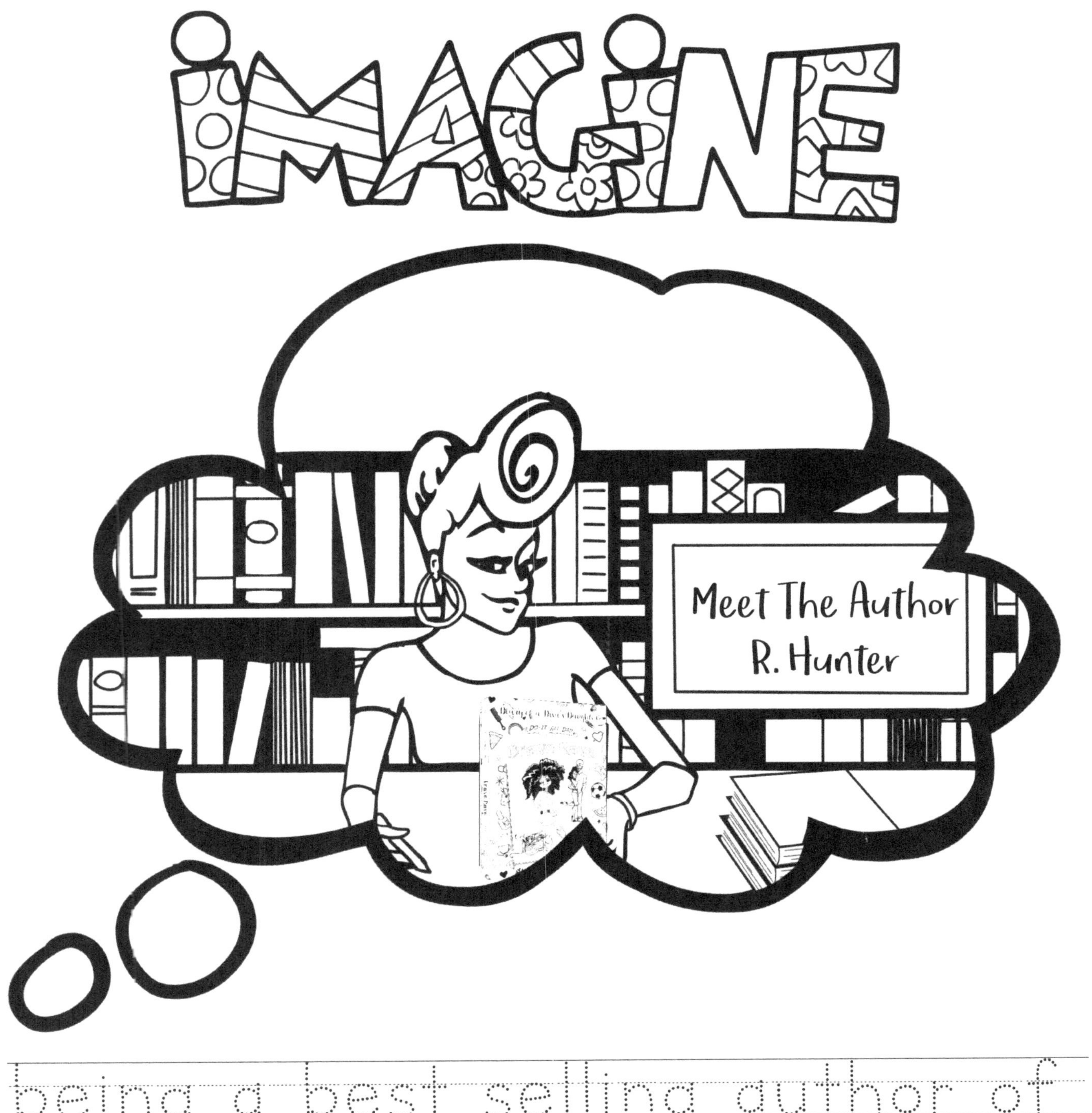

being a best selling author of
books that share great stories
that inspire the world.

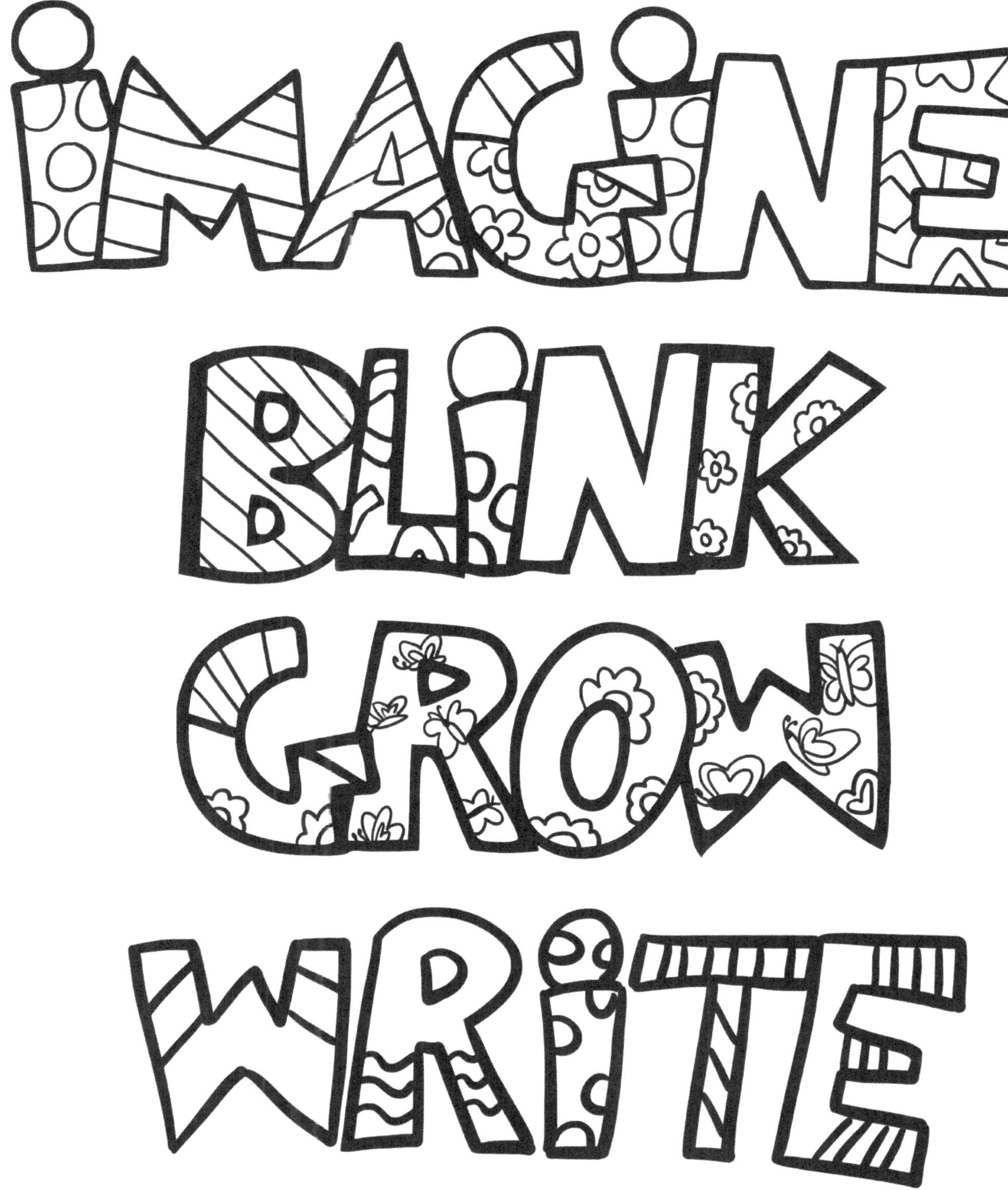
IMAGINE
BLINK
GROW
WRITE

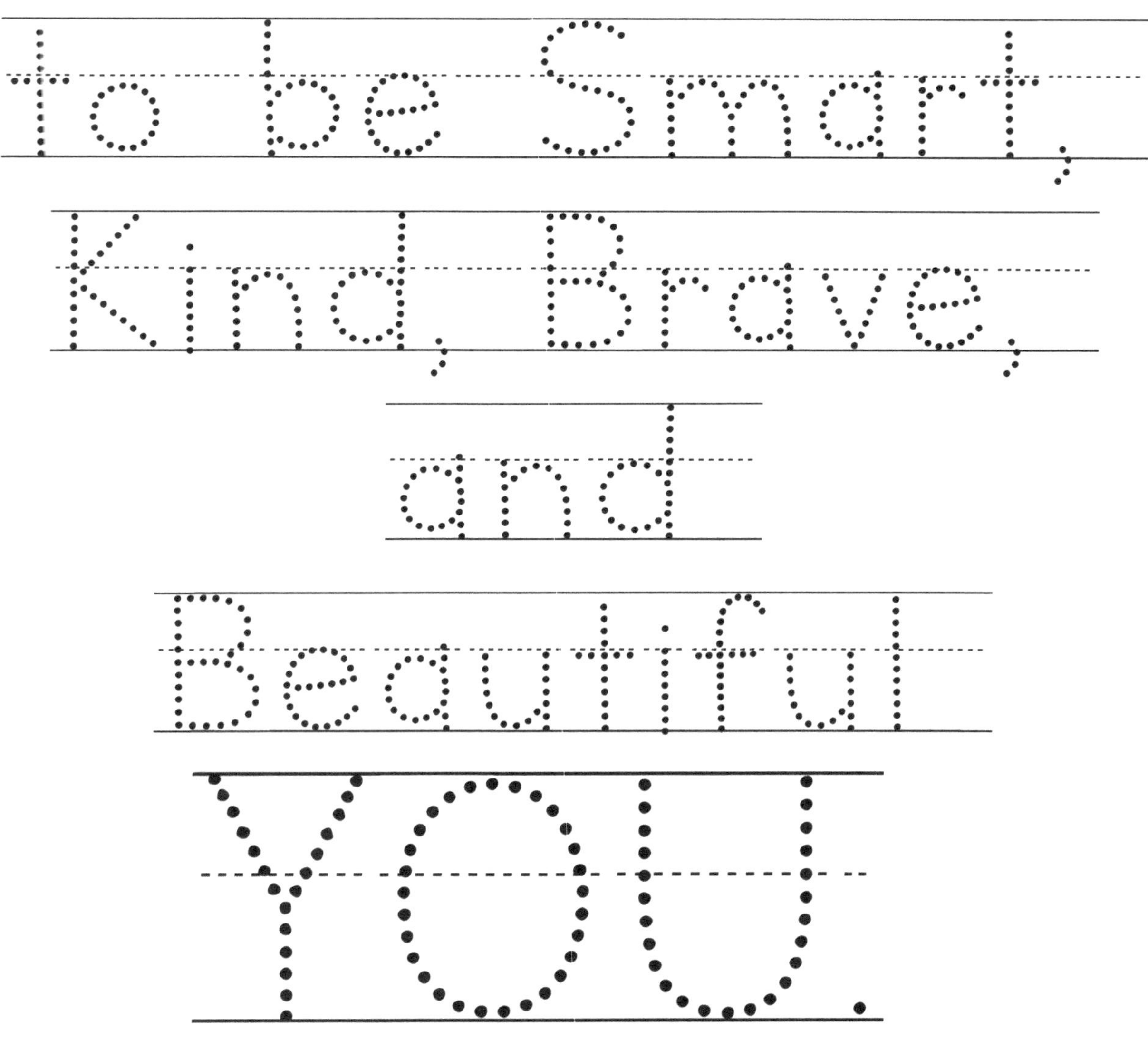

to be Smart,
Kind, Brave,
and
Beautiful
YOU.

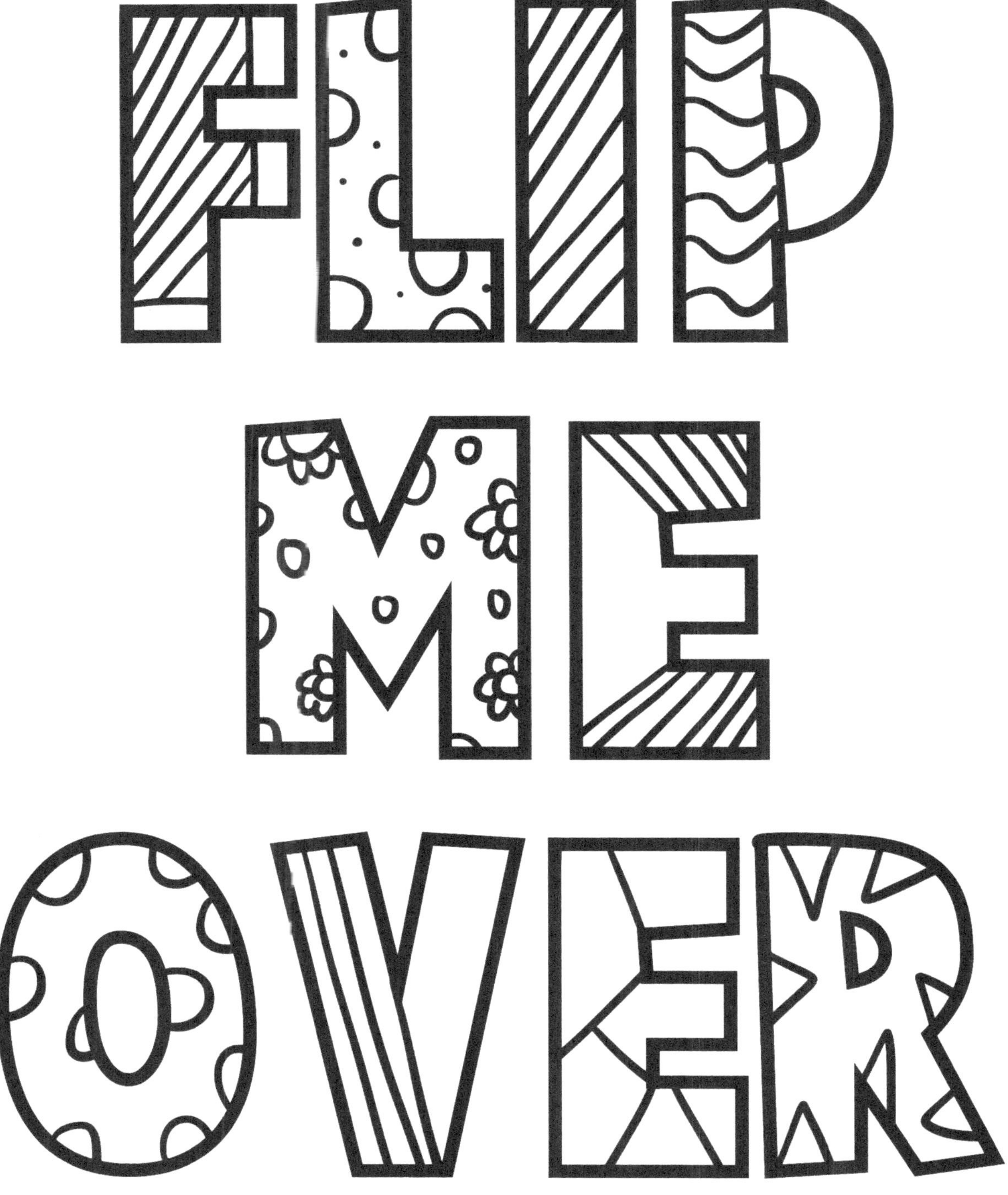
FLIP
ME
OVER